Woodturning
for
Cabinetmakers

Woodturning
for
Cabinetmakers

Michael Dunbar

 Sterling Publishing Co., Inc.   New York

DEDICATION
To Mercedes

Library of Congress Cataloging-in-Publication Data

Dunbar, Michael.
    Woodturning for cabinetmakers / by Michael Dunbar.
        p.   cm.
    Includes bibliographical references and index.
    1. Turning.   I. Title.
  TT203.D86   1990
  684′.083—dc20   90-46055
                                   CIP

10 9 8 7 6 5 4 3 2 1

© 1990 by Michael Dunbar
Published by Sterling Publishing Company, Inc.
387 Park Avenue South, New York, N.Y. 10016
Distributed in Canada by Sterling Publishing
% Canadian Manda Group, P.O. Box 920, Station U
Toronto, Ontario, Canada M8Z 5P9
Distributed in Great Britain and Europe by Cassell PLC
Villiers House, 41/47 Strand, London WC2N 5JE, England
Distributed in Australia by Capricorn Ltd.
P.O. Box 665, Lane Cove, NSW 2066
Manufactured in the United States of America
All rights reserved

Sterling ISBN 0-8069-6700-5

Contents

INTRODUCTION

The craft of working wood in a lathe is called turning. The people who do this work are called turners. Woodturning is an ancient craft that was practiced by most early civilizations. It was also a widespread craft. Most cultures produced large numbers of turners, and there was a great demand for their products.

Up until only several generations ago, turners in all western countries earned their living making the turned wooden products needed by the rest of society. Turners were considered an essential part of society, and were well-respected. Furthermore, these craftsmen were so accomplished that the term "made in a lathe" was used to describe anything that was cleverly and nicely executed.

Turning was different from many other woodworking trades in that turners did not usually make completed products. They did make some turned items that they sold directly to the consumer. These included such things as walking sticks, bowls, and other small utilitarian household goods that used to be called "treenware," a corruption of the words "tree ware." (See Illus. 1.) Most of the time, however, a turner made parts that were used by other woodworkers, principally furniture makers and builders.

There were reasons for this. Although turners were woodworkers, turning is a separate and distinct craft that demands particular skills and knowledge. In this way, it is very much like carving or marquetry. Carpenters, joiners, and cabinetmakers were all skilled craftsmen who needed turnings for their work, but they did not necessarily need to be able to turn.

There is another reason why turning was a distinct part of woodworking. Turning requires a large machine called a lathe. A lathe has always been an expensive piece of equipment. Furthermore, the lathe could not be easily disassembled and stored, so even when it was not being used, it still required its own space. Space has always been at a premium in crowded workshops. As a result, even though

Illus. 1. Traditionally, turners made few products that could be sold directly to customers. Most of those retail products were everyday utilitarian objects known as "treenware," or sometimes just "treen." The treenware shown here are a mortar and pestle, a hand mirror, a darning egg, a herb crusher, a spigot, a bowl, a rolling pin, and a set of clothespins.

the woodworkers who built buildings or made furniture regularly used turnings in their work, they did not necessarily own a lathe, or know how to use one. They instead depended on turners.

Woodturners supplied the building trades with many products, including newel posts and balusters (the upright turnings under stair banisters), porch columns, roof balustrades, rosettes, corner blocks, and other architectural details. For furniture makers, turners produced the legs for chairs, tables, and case pieces, bedposts, and even drawer pulls. Most of these parts are long and thin, and they were spindle-turned. Spindle turning is done with the wood secured between the lathe's two centers.

After the mid 18th century, perhaps the largest consumer of turnings was the turned or common chair industry. Common chairs include Windsor, ladder-back, and Fancy (Hitchcock-type) chairs. These chairs were inexpensive, and were most often used in the kitchen. They are all still made today.

While parts for formal (expensive) chairs were usually cut and shaped with saws and planes, the majority of the components in turned chairs were made in a lathe. Old chairmaker's records dating from a time when most woodworking was still done by hand indicate that chairmakers purchased chair parts from turners in lots that had many thousands of pieces.

Besides doing predominantly spindle turning, old-time turners also made turnings that were used in sets. For example, they might make any of the following: a row of balusters, four table legs, the legs for a set of chairs, a pair of porch columns, or a set of drawer pulls. This indicates that besides knowing how to turn, a turner also knew how to duplicate the part—make the same part over and over again.

Both the craft of woodturning and the turners who practice it have changed dramatically over the past couple of generations. Today, the building, furniture, and chair industries still consume large numbers of identical turned parts. However, the old skills are no longer necessary because spindle-turned parts are now made in factories on tracer and back-knife lathes. The people who operate these machines, while still called turners, are really machine operators rather than highly skilled craftsmen. Their job now consists of knowing how to chuck up a wooden blank and how to turn on the machine. When the cutting is done, they turn off the lathe, remove the turning, and chuck up another piece. This job is a far cry from the skills once possessed by hand turners.

In spite of these mass-production turning factories, much of the lost handicraft of woodturning has been revived over the past two decades (as have many other branches of woodworking), and turning is now widely practiced by both professional and amateur turners alike. These modern craftspeople are very different from the machine operators who work in turning factories in that they are every bit as skilled as the old-time woodturners. In fact, in some ways they are even more talented.

However, during this revival, hand turning took on a new emphasis. Modern turners are more artistic than craft-oriented, and as artists they are more interested in giving expression through their understanding of wood than they are in making purely functional objects. In fact, many of their pieces are intended to be looked at and not used. As a result, modern turners no longer work as subcontractors providing their products to other crafts. Instead, they largely focus on making complete turned objects that stand alone, such as bowls, vases, platters, etc. (See Illus. 2.)

Modern turning also differs from old-time turning in that turners no longer make large numbers of the same object. In other words, they do not do a lot of duplication. Many of the objects made by today's turners are unique one-of-a-kind items. Although today's turners may work for a while on a certain design or type of turned object, they are usually exploring new ideas, not duplicating.

There is also another difference between old-time turning and modern turning. Old-time turned objects were inexpensive (for ex-

Illus. 2. Today's turners are both highly skilled technicians and artists who use turning as a means of expression. They generally specialize in one-of-a-kind, freestanding objects that are usually faceplate-turned. The pieces shown here are by California artist/turner Howard Luin.

ample, the turned parts for the turned chair industry). Most of the objects made by today's turners are very expensive, selling for prices that will make the uninitiated gasp with disbelief.

Modern turning also contrasts with old-time woodturning in one additional way. Most modern woodturning is done using a faceplate or other special chucks that hold the object. Most of the furniture and building parts produced by old-time turners were spindle-turned. This shift from spindle turning inexpensive, functional, duplicate parts, to faceplate-turning expensive one-of-a-kind, non-functional objects is reflected in most of the books written about the subject and in the many seminars that are held around the country. Most writers and teachers stress the skills used in modern woodturning over those of the traditional craft.

Modern woodturning's emphasis has had an influence on the furniture and buildings that are being designed today. Though there are still many talented furniture makers and builders they are not well-informed about the craft of woodturning. As a result, turnings are not used as commonly as they were in the past. Parts such as table legs or stair balusters are more likely to be made with a table saw or router rather than turned in a lathe.

This lack of experience working on the lathe also handicaps those craftsmen who make re-

productions. They tend to focus on the Queen Anne and Chippendale periods when the cabriole leg (ending in either a pad foot, or a claw and ball) was fashionable. Cabriole legs are cut out with a band saw and shaped with spokeshaves and carving tools, so turning skills are not needed to reproduce pieces from these periods. Similarly, when reproducers make Federal period furniture they tend to focus on the Hepplewhite style, which emphasized tapered legs. The Sheraton style is not as popular with reproducers, since these pieces require turnings, which they often cannot easily make.

My hope is that this book will begin to change this situation. Its purpose is to acquaint woodworkers, especially furniture makers and builders, with spindle turning so that they can learn to make parts for their woodworking.

Thus, this book has a very specific focus, and is not intended to be a general book about woodturning. It differs from most other books that have been written about turning, in that just one chapter examines faceplate work (which can be used to make a few parts, such as tops for small tables). The main emphasis is on spindle turning and the various techniques used to make parts.

If you want to include turnings in your work, you have to be able to duplicate parts. After all, few pieces of furniture or architecture require just a single turning (four legs are generally used on most pieces of furniture, and a staircase can have 50 balusters). Thus, this book also stresses duplication. It not only shows you how to make turned parts, it teaches you how to make sets of them. I will also explain some special techniques that old turners used to decorate the turned parts they made for builders and furniture makers. These techniques include reeding, fluting, and spiral turning.

As a woodworker, you have probably developed a considerable number of skills, some of which required years to learn. Most of them will not be of much value to you in turning (except the ability to sharpen), as turning is substantially different from other types of woodworking. Fortunately, it does not require a long time to learn the basic spindle-turning techniques that you need to make turned furniture and building parts.

As you make your first attempts on the lathe, you can hardly imagine how fast and precise an accomplished turner can work. If you ever have the occasion to watch someone with a lot of experience (one way is to rent or buy a videotape), you will be surprised at the speed and confidence exhibited by an accomplished wood turner.

When I was in business as a woodworker, I specialized in making Windsor chairs. Windsor chairs are turned chairs. Fifty to 60 percent of their parts are made in a lathe. Since I only turned half a day a week, I never developed the same speed as does someone who turns every day. However, I was still fast enough to turn 8 baluster chair legs in an hour.

You too can become an accomplished woodturner. This book will provide the groundwork of information you need to get started, and will guide you past some of the problems you may encounter. With this information and through practice you will soon be working comfortably with the lathe and with turning tools.

1

EXPLORING THE LATHE

You need a lathe to make turnings. There is no other option. Without a table saw, you can still saw by hand. If you do not have a thickness planer, you can always surface a board with hand planes. Most of the jobs done with a router can also be done with other tools. However, to turn, you need a lathe.

The lathe is perhaps the oldest of all woodworking machines. In both concept and in operation it is so like the potter's wheel that you have to wonder if that device was not the inspiration for the lathe.

One fundamental difference between the lathe and most other woodworking machinery is that the lathe does not itself act upon the wood. It spins an unworked piece of wood called a blank. You shape the blank with a variety of chisel-like tools. For these reasons, most turners usually think of the lathe as a tool, rather than a woodworking machine.

Illus. 1-1. To make turnings, you need a lathe—one of the oldest machines known to Man. This one was made by Conover Woodcraft Specialties, Inc., of Ohio.

Parts and Characteristics of the Lathe

HEADSTOCK

A lathe consists of several major parts. If you were to stand in front of a lathe, the upright element you would note on your left is the *headstock*. It is responsible for turning the wood and regulating the speed at which it spins (known as revolutions per minute or RPMs). The headstock contains a central horizontal shaft or spindle. This shaft usually has a pulley(s) mounted on it. This pulley is connected by belts to the power source, generally an electric motor. (See Illus. 1-2.)

The headstock's spindle is usually hollow. On the right end is a fixture called the *drive center*. If you wish to remove the drive center to look at it, insert a drift (a long metal rod) into the far end of the spindle. Strike the drift. The center will pop loose. Be ready to catch it so it is not damaged by a fall. (See Illus. 1-3.)

The most common type of drive center is called a *spur center*. The head of the spur center has two or four spurs with sharpened edges that bite into the wood and drive the blank. (See Illus 1-3.) The spurs also prevent slippage caused by the counterforce of the turning tool.

Note that at the intersection of the spurs there is a small, sharp point. This is the exact center of the spur center, and it is one end of the axis on which the wood revolves. If before mounting the blank in the lathe you make a mark that locates the blank's center, this point will be pressed into that mark.

The right end of the headstock's hollow spindle is reverse-tapered. If you insert your finger into the spindle, you can feel this. The drive center's shank is also reverse-tapered and forms a truncated cone. The center's and spindle's angle of taper falls within a narrow range of angles that are called locking tapers. This means that when these two parts (the tapered shank and hollow spindle) are pressed together, friction causes them to grab securely. Locking tapers are designated by the names of the companies that first made them, and are usually distinguished by numbers. Morse #1 and Morse #2 are perhaps the most common.

The only way to break the friction in a lock-

Illus. 1-2. The headstock is the upright element that drives the wood and regulates the speed at which it spins. It has a horizontal central shaft mounted with a pulley. The pulley is connected to a motor by a belt.

Illus. 1-3. The drive center is usually removed with a drift inserted into the far end of the spindle. Catch the drive center in your hand. If it falls, it could be damaged.

Illus. 1-4. A spur center has four (sometimes just two) spurs whose sharpened edges are driven into the end of the blank. At the intersection of the spurs is a point which you can remove by loosening an Allen screw.

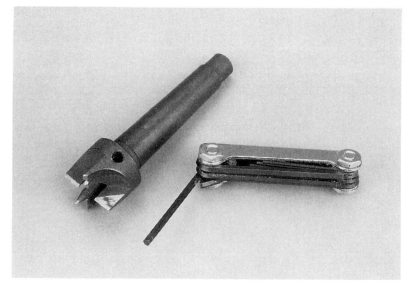

ing taper, or to release its grip is by shock. This too, usually can be done by inserting a metal rod, called a drift, into the left end of the hollow spindle. Butt the drift against the rear end of the center's shank and rap it with a hammer. The taper's self-locking action will break, and the drive center will loosen.

The headstock's spindle is usually threaded on both ends. These threads permit faceplates and other fixtures to be attached for either inboard or outboard turning. Faceplates and their uses are discussed in Chapter 15.

The headstock usually has a removable cover that permits access to the drive belts and pulleys so that you can change their adjustments and the speed at which the lathe spins. When the lathe is operating, the cover should always be securely in place for your protection.

TAIL STOCK

Note that another upright element is located at the right-hand end of the lathe. This is called the tail stock. (See Illus. 1-5.) Like the headstock, the tail stock also has a horizontal hollow spindle. The left end of this spindle has a second center. This is the tail center. There are two different types of tail centers: live and dead centers.

There are two types of dead centers. The first is a simple polished metal fixture that is tapered on both ends. (See Illus. 1-6.) As on the drive center, the shank end is also a locking taper which usually has the same manufacturer's system and number as the drive center. In other words, if your lathe has a #2 Morse taper-drive center, it will usually have a #2 Morse taper-tail center.

The taper on the other end of the dead center is shorter and more blunt (60 degrees). It terminates in a sharp point, which under pressure makes a deep dimple in the end of the blank. The very tip of this point is also one end of the axis on which the blank revolves. (Remember, the point in the drive center is the other end.) If you have located the blank's center on both of its ends, this 60-degree point will also be pressed into one of those marks when you chuck the blank in the lathe.

Illus. 1-5. The tail stock is the upright element at the right-hand end of the lathe. You can move it back and forth on the bed to adjust it for the length of the blank you are turning. The tail stock also has a center, which you can advance or retract by turning a crank or (as in this case) a wheel. This allows you to both grip and remove a piece of wood.

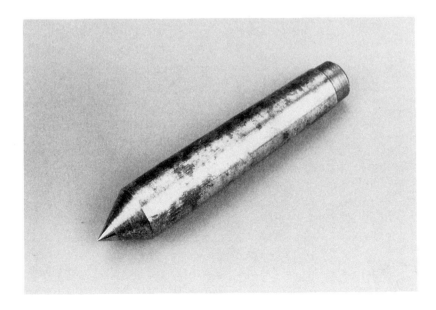

Illus. 1-6. Different types of centers can be used on the tail stock. Shown here is a 60-degree dead center. It is inexpensive, but because it does not turn with the wood, it creates friction and heat.

The second type of dead center is the cup center. (See Illus. 1-7.) This device also has a locking tapered shank, but instead of a 60-degree taper, the other end has a small center point surrounded by a raised ring. The ring's outside edge is bevelled, so that it bites more easily into the end grain.

Both types of dead centers (60 degrees and cup) have disadvantages. They are stationary and do not spin. The blank spins on the dead center, and even though the metal surface is polished, friction still results. If you do not complete the turning quickly, the area of wood in contact with the center will heat until it begins to smoke. In time, that spot will char and will eventually turn into charcoal. You can minimize the heat buildup by putting a lubricant such as petroleum jelly or wax on the cen-

ter. However, both these lubricants liquefy and penetrate the wood, which can cause problems later when you are adding a finish.

Both types of dead centers are relatively inexpensive. They are most useful for simple turnings that can be done very quickly.

The other type of tail center is called a live or ball-bearing center (See Illus. 1-8.) These centers are referred to as live because they spin with the blank. Use a live center on a complicated turning that will take more than several minutes to complete.

There are two types of live centers: a small, 60-degree point, and a cup center. Both types are fixed in a hub that contains the ball bearings and races.

Because live centers are far more complicated to manufacture than dead centers, they

Illus. 1-7. Another alternative is the cup center, which is also a dead center. It is the best choice when you are turning small parts, as the raised ring helps prevents splitting. You can also remove the cup center's point by loosening an Allen screw. (Tools courtesy of Woodcraft Supply)

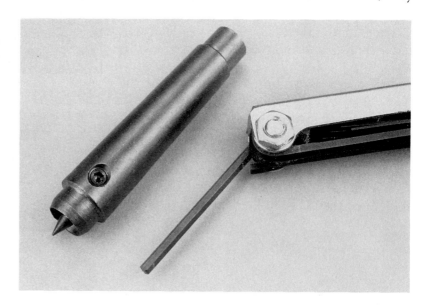

Illus. 1-8. A live center spins with the wood, eliminating friction. The large hub contains the bearings. Live centers are more expensive than dead centers.

are more expensive. However, if you plan on making complex turnings that take a lot of time, a live center is well worth the cost.

As explained above, both live centers and dead centers are available with a 60-degree point. The end in contact with the billet is a squat, polished steel cone which has to be pressed about 3/16 inch into the end of the blank. This will leave a dimple in the end of the finished turning, also about 3/16 inch across.

Because the 60-degree point pushes so far into the end of a blank, it is most suitable for heavy turnings which have to be gripped securely. However, if you are making small delicate parts, the blunt 60-degree point may split the wood. So, instead use a cup center. This point is much smaller than the 60-degree point, and creates less splitting force. Also, the raised ring holds the wood together, resisting the point's splitting action.

The back of the tail stock's spindle has a wheel or a crank that when turned advances or retracts the spindle. This allows you to grip the blank tightly between the two centers as well as remove the completed turning. However, advancing the spindle counterclockwise all the way will eventually pull apart the grip of the spindle's locking taper. This is how the center is removed, rather than with a drift.

The tail stock also has a lock for the spindle (the handle is usually on the top of the casting). Once the tail center has been advanced to grip the blank, this lock is set to keep the spindle's setting from loosening as a result of vibration.

Unlike the headstock (which is normally in a fixed position), the tail stock is movable and slides back and forth to permit you to adjust the lathe to the length of the wooden blank you are turning. To move the tail stock, you first have to loosen a second lock, the one that secures the tail stock in place on the bed. The lock is controlled by a second handle, often located in a cavity in the tail stock, or on its front surface.

LATHE BED

The headstock and the tail stock are attached to the lathe bed. Usually the bed is a long, narrow body of cast iron with two machined surfaces called ways. There is a narrow gap between the ways. The tail stock and rest move along this gap. On some lathes, the bed can be a metal tube or a pair of parallel tubes. On early lathes, the bed was made of wood. It was replaced with cast iron during the Industrial Revolution. It is interesting that the traditional wood-bed lathe has come full circle, and that a manufacturer again offers a lathe that uses one. This lathe is called the Conover lathe.

LATHE CAPACITY

Once you are familiar with the head and tail stock and the bed, you can better understand the measurements that are known as the lathe's capacity. All lathes have two capacities. The first is the distance between the center and the bed. This capacity is also called the *swing*. (See Chapter 15.) The swing determines how large a diameter of turning can be made on the lathe.

The second capacity is the maximum distance you can move the tail center away from the drive center. This capacity regulates how long a blank you can turn. Most lathe beds will allow a maximum distance between centers of about 33 inches. This is long enough for table and chair legs, but is much too short for most bedposts, the stiles of ladder-back chairs, and many architectural parts. Longer lathes are still made, but are more expensive than shorter ones. Six- and 8-foot-long bed lathes are sometimes available second hand, but can require a lot of work to be put back into operation. One of the virtues of a wooden bed is that being a woodworker, you can make it any length you want.

STAND

The lathe bed is elevated to a comfortable working height by a stand which usually consists of a pair of legs, often made of cast iron. However, in many small shops (where space is at a premium) the lathe is sometimes mounted on a bench. I personally do not like this arrangement, as it is more difficult to clean around (turning makes lots of shavings that make frequent cleaning necessary). Also, some operations are easier if you can work from both sides of the lathe. These operations include spiral-turning, reeding, and fluting.

TOOL REST

When you are turning, the wooden blank is driven against your tools with considerable force. The tool is supported on a sturdy horizontal surface called a tool rest. (See Illus. 1-9.) This prevents it from being knocked around.

The tool rest is usually shaped like the letter T, except that the horizontal surface is much longer that the vertical stem. The horizontal

Illus. 1-9. The tool rest supports the tools to prevent them from being knocked about by the spinning blank. Note that the rest's height can be adjusted by turning a knob located on its front. This also allows the rest to be pivoted. You can adjust the rest's placement on the bed by loosening a handle (or, in this case, a wheel placed under the bed).

surface supports the tool when you are turning, while the vertical stem is gripped in a sliding bracket that sits on the bed's ways.

The tool rest bracket is attached directly to the bed. It slides between the head and tail stocks. Like the tail stock, the tool rest bracket also has two locks. The first lock grips the rest's vertical stem and, when loosened, allows you to change the rest's height. This lock is usually on the front of the bracket where it is easily accessible.

The second lock secures the bracket in position on the bed. When it is loosened, the bracket can be moved along the bed and also rotated in relation to the axis of the centers. This feature is helpful when you are doing inboard faceplate turning, a process that is described in Chapter 15.

SOURCES OF POWER

Most lathes are powered by an electric motor, although I have an Amish friend in Ohio who runs his with a gasoline engine. Historically, many other sources of power have been used. The most basic was human muscle. Sometimes the muscle power came from the turner's own leg as he pumped a treadle attached to a fly wheel. (See Illus. 1-10.) This type of muscle-powered machine is called a treadle lathe.

Another muscle-powered lathe was the great wheel. This lathe had a large wooden wheel with a crank handle attached to the hub. The crank was turned by an apprentice.

The spring pole lathe is another type of treadle lathe. It too relies on the user's muscle power. (See Illus. 1-11.) This machine is about as basic as a lathe can be. It is called a spring pole because it makes use of the natural springiness of a green sapling. The pole is bent over a fulcrum to create tension. A rope is tied to the end of the pole, is then looped around the blank, and is finally attached to a treadle. As the treadle is pumped, it pulls down the pole. When the treadle is released, the pole returns to its former position. Each time the treadle is depressed, the blank spins and can be

Illus. 1-10. Before the development of the electric motor, lathes were often driven by a treadle, pumped by the turner's foot. This treadle lathe was made by Charles Pace of Houston, Texas, who is also shown operating it. (Photo courtesy of Hugh Lenox Scott)

Illus. 1-11. The oldest and simplest form of lathe is the spring pole, which takes advantage of the natural suppleness of a green sapling. This one was made by its user, Don Weber.

shaped with the lathe tools. Unfortunately, as the pole pulls the treadle back into its upright position, it spins the blank in the opposite direction from the one required for cutting. This means that a turner working on a spring pole lathe is not working 50 percent of the time. As inefficient as this sounds, English spring-pole lathe turners (called bodgers) were remarkably fast. Reportedly, a bodger working on a spring pole lathe could produce a Windsor chair leg every two minutes.

In the past, water wheels and steam have also been used to drive lathes. During the early 19th century a woodturner named George Walker worked in Portsmouth, New Hampshire, the city where I live. Mr. Walker's shop was set up over a tidal inlet. He advertised that he used the power of seawater flowing through the inlet to drive his lathe. He made note of the fact that his water wheel was reversible, and, as a result, he could turn at all times of the day no matter which way the tide was running.

In all cases (except for the spring pole), the lathe's power source is connected to the headstock pulley by some form of belt, usually either a flat or V belt. (See Illus. 1-12.)

Illus. 1-12. The headstock's spindle is usually driven by a belt connected to an electric motor. You can increase or decrease the speed of the lathe by changing the arrangement of the pulleys.

SPEED

The speed at which a lathe turns can usually be adjusted. Some lathes have a dial or handle which when turned automatically adjusts the lathe's pulleys, making it possible for you to select any speed without having to shut off the lathe. However, the speed of a lathe is usually changed by moving the belt from pulley to pulley (there are pulleys of several different diameters on both the headstock spindle and the motor's shaft). Pages 62 and 63 describe how to adjust a lathe's speed and how to calculate its RPMs.

INDEX HEAD

An index head is another useful feature often found on a wood lathe. (See Illus. 1-13.) The index head divides a circle into even segments—halves, quarters, eighths, sixteenths, etc. It allows you to quickly and accurately divide a turning's surface into equal segments, facilitating such jobs as reeding. (See Chapter 12.) An index head is generally mounted on the headstock spindle. How to use the index head is described on pages 135 and 136.

Illus. 1-13. An index head allows you to divide a turning into equal horizontal segments, facilitating such operations as reeding and fluting.

Selecting a Lathe

Being familiar with the lathe helps you to determine what to look for when buying one. Avoid poorly designed lathes that have locks and handles in awkward places. If you use these types of lathes, your speed and efficiency will be greatly reduced. Before buying a lathe, look it over to make sure that it is a machine on which you can work easily and efficiently.

Make sure that you buy a lathe that is capable of meeting the demands you will place on it.

A cheap lathe is next to useless—never buy one. If you expect to be doing a lot of turning or to be making large turnings, do not buy a lightweight lathe.

Also, beware of forsaking a durable lathe for one with many features. The additional fixtures and options will never compensate for the lathe's lack of strength. In fact, if given a choice between a very basic, but heavy-duty lathe and a more lightweight one with lots of fixtures and features, I would take the durable lathe every time.

2
LATHE TOOLS

Selecting Tools

Most novice turners have two major misconceptions about lathe tools. First, someone who has not worked on the lathe imagines turning to be a herculean struggle between himself and the wood, in which he is required to be armed with hefty tools. Second, novice turners assume that in order to do a wide variety of turnings they need a wide variety of tools.

Tool catalogues reinforce the latter misconception by displaying a vast array of turning chisels. Just open a recent catalogue and you will note the mind-boggling selection of turning tools offered. Unless you know what you are looking at, you will quickly become confused.

There is one important point to bear in mind when pondering the vast selection of tools available. Many of the tools offered for sale will not be useful to you as long as you are turning between centers. For this reason, do not buy a great number of tools right away. Also, do not buy boxed sets of tools. These, too, will contain tools that you will not often need.

In fact, once you have become more experienced on the lathe, you will be surprised at how few lathe tools you do use. Since turning tools are expensive, buying tools you do not need can turn out to be a very costly lesson.

Start off by buying only a few basic tools and learn to use them. As you become more skilled, you will be able to determine what additional tools you need. Over the years, I have turned all sorts of projects, but still only use five or six tools. My early mistakes are stored in a drawer.

The following tools are useful for most beginners: a ¾-inch roughing gouge, a ¾- and a ¼-inch spindle (lady finger) gouge, a ½- and a ¾-inch skew, and a ³⁄₁₆-inch parting tool. (See Illus. 2-1.) A 1¼-inch roughing gouge, a ½-inch spindle gouge, and a ¼-inch skew can be bought later if you find that you need them. A further description of all these tools is given below.

Types of Turning Tools

Turning tools are similar to chisels. They are longer and thicker than most chisels, the extra strength being necessary to resist the shock and stress caused by the spinning wood.

Turning tools also have longer handles. These handles provide a surer grip, which prevents the tool from being knocked about by the spinning blank. They also give you greater control. When you make a cut, you often pivot the tool on the tool rest. The cutting end of the tool extends only a short distance over the tool rest. Extending over the other side of the tool rest is the remainder of the tool blade and its handle. This combined length is approximately 10 to 20 times greater than the end that is cutting.

This difference in length means that in order to move the cutting edge a certain distance, you have to move the handle a far greater amount. This results in good control of the cutting edge. This concept is similar to that used for adjustment knobs. Some adjustment knobs are geared down and have to be turned many times to achieve a small amount of movement.

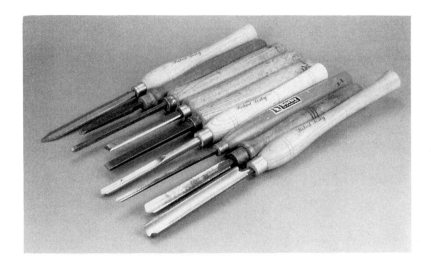

Illus. 2-1. These are the lathe tools that I use. From front to back, they are: a ¾-inch roughing gouge; a ¾-inch spindle gouge; a ¼-inch "lady finger" gouge; a ½-inch spindle gouge; ¾-, ½- and ¼-inch skews; a ½-inch diamond point; and a ³⁄₁₆-inch parting tool.

Just as gearing-down results in more precision, so does the long handle and blade.

Following is a description of the various lathe tools most commonly used to make furniture and architectural parts. How they are ground and sharpened is the subject of the next chapter.

GOUGES

The tools most closely identified with turning are gouges. You probably have experience with bench gouges and carving gouges from the woodworking you have done at the bench. As with these tools, a turning gouge's cross section is an arc. Gouges used on the bench are made with different arcs, called sweeps. The same is

true of turning chisels, only their arcs are called flutes.

Turning gouges are made with just two flutes (bench gouges have three, while carving gouges have up to 10). These flutes are designated as either standard (also called shallow) flutes or deep flutes. (See Illus. 2-2.)

ROUGHING GOUGE

When you chuck a blank in your lathe, the first step is to make it round. This should be done as quickly as possible. This process is called roughing (or rough rounding), and it is done with a roughing (also called a roughing out) gouge.

Illus. 2-2. At left is a standard or shallow gouge, and at right a deep flute gouge.

Illus. 2-3. A roughing gouge's cutting edge is ground straight across, while the edges of spindle gouges are rounded like your fingernails.

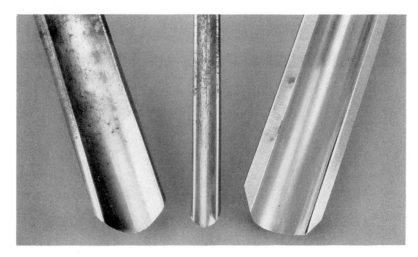

A roughing gouge is a heavy tool well suited for the fast removal of waste wood. It is a deep flute gouge that has its cutting edge ground straight across in the same manner as bench and carving gouges. (See Illus. 2-3.)

In use, a roughing gouge cuts a deep trough out of the corners of the spinning blank. At the same time, the cutting edge's straight sides completely sever the chip, so there is little or no tearout from the surrounding wood. Although the roughing gouge is a very aggressive tool that cuts a thick chip, at the same time it keeps the process under control.

Roughing gouges come in different sizes. You can determine the size of a gouge by measuring across the blade's open upper surface. I use a ¾-inch roughing gouge for general work and a 1¼-inch roughing gouge for heavy work. Heavy work is work that requires 2-inch thick or thicker turning squares.

SPINDLE GOUGES

Spindle gouges usually have lighter blades than roughing gouges, and have standard flutes. Like roughing gouges, spindle gouges come in different sizes. These sizes are also determined by measuring across the blade. I use a ¼-, ½-, and ¾-inch spindle gouge.

Rather than being used to round the blank (although they can do this on light work), spindle gouges are used to shape the various elements that make up a turning. As a result, there is no single purpose for any individual gouge. Each is used where and when it is the appropriate tool, and when you are comfortable using it. You learn when to use a spindle gouge only through practice. For example, I often use my ¾-inch spindle gouge for roughrounding small pieces.

A spindle gouge's cutting edge is rounded so that it looks like a fingernail. In fact, the colloquial name for a small spindle gouge is "lady finger" gouge. (See Illus. 2-3.) The round cutting edge is necessary, as the corners created by a straight edge could catch in the end grain when you are cutting coves and other concave shapes.

SKEWS

The skew is a flat chisel with dual bezels, one ground on each side of the wide blade. The bench chisels used for woodworking have a single bezel. The cutting edge is formed by the intersection of the sloping bezel and the flat upper surface. Thus, the cutting edge is aligned with one side of the blade.

The skew is very different from bench chisels. Its edge is formed by the intersection of its two bezels, and the edge is aligned with the blade's center. (See Illus. 2-4 and 2-5.)

A skew is also different from a bench chisel

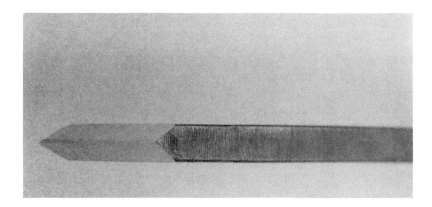

Illus. 2-4. The cutting edge of a skew is formed by two bezels, and is aligned with the blade's center.

Illus. 2-5. The cutting edge of a skew is also angled at about 75 degrees to the blade's edge.

in that its cutting edge is not square to the sides of the blade. Instead, it is angled at about 75 degrees to the blade's edges. When such a sloping cutting edge occurs on any tool, it is said to be skewed, or askew, hence the name of this type of turning tool.

Where the skewed cutting edge meets the blade's edges, it creates two angled corners. The one at an acute angle is called the toe. The toe is generally considered the upper end of the cutting edge. The other corner—at an obtuse angle—is the heel. The heel is usually considered the bottom of the cutting edge.

The skew is perhaps the most difficult turning tool to learn to use properly, but it is also the most versatile. The more accomplished the woodturner, the more he relies on his skews for roughing, paring and planing (finishing). All of these techniques will be explained later.

Skews come in a variety of different sizes, which are determined by measuring across the blade's width. I own and use three skews: a ¼-, ½- and ¾-inch skew.

PARTING TOOL

There are currently a number of new types of parting tools being sold. The purpose of these new parting tools is to eliminate ragged corners that sometimes occur on a parting cut. I have not used any of these newly designed tools, and so cannot write about them with any authority. Instead, I have always been satisfied with the traditional type of parting tool. The cross section of this traditional parting tool is shaped like an elongated diamond. Indeed, it is called a diamond-section parting tool by its manufacturer.

Like the skew, the parting tool also has two bezels, but they are ground on the blade's narrow edges, rather than the wide sides. The cutting edge is located in the middle of the tool where the two bezels intersect. (See Illus. 2-6.) This location also corresponds to the thick rib running down the middle of the blade. As a result, the cutting edge occurs on the blade where it is the thickest.

Illus. 2-6. The parting tool also has two bezels, but they are ground on the blade's narrow edges. This aligns the cutting edge with the thick rib running down the middle of the blade.

When a deep parting cut is being made, the relieved edges are not in contact with the wood. This reduces the amount of friction, as well as the possibility of damage to the turning.

The parting tool makes a plunge cut. It is set on the tool rest and pushed forward into the wood at a right angle to the axis of the blank. The parting tool is used for dividing a blank into segments (which are then shaped with other tools), for establishing depths, and for cutting pieces out of the lathe. (See Chapter 5.)

Parting tools come in different sizes, which are determined by measuring the blade at its thickest point. I use a ³⁄₁₆-inch diamond-section parting tool.

DIAMOND POINT

Like the skew, the diamond or spear point, is a very versatile tool. It can be used to take a clean slice off the end of a detail (such as a square), leaving a glassy, smooth surface on the end grain. It can also be used for planing small surfaces, just as you would do with a skew. Finally, its pointed end can make V grooves.

Like the skew and parting tool, a diamond point also has two bezels. (See Illus. 2-7.) However, both are ground onto the same surface of the blade and placed 110 degrees (or less) from each other. This produces a pointed end. Thus, unlike the skew and parting tool, which have just one cutting edge formed by the intersection of their two bezels, the diamond point has two cutting edges, one where each of the two bezels meets the blade's flat upper surface.

Illus. 2-7. The diamond point also has two bezels, but they are ground on the same side of the blade and placed at a 90-degree angle to each other.

MEASURING TOOLS

When you are turning, you do the actual cutting with the tools just described. However, you use measuring tools to determine where and how deep to cut. Following is an exploration of the different types of measuring tools.

Calipers

Calipers are used for measuring the diameter of a turning. (See Illus. 2-8.) Most turnings have more than one diameter, so you should own several pairs of calipers. When you are making a set of turnings, you can adjust each pair of calipers to a particular measurement, and use them all throughout the job without changing them. Thus, owning several calipers is easier and less complicated than changing the setting on a single pair every time you make a new measurement. Also, having a pair of calipers adjusted for a certain measurement makes mistakes less likely. The pairs of calipers you own should be of different sizes, as most turnings have larger and smaller diameters.

DIVIDERS

Like calipers, dividers are used for measuring.

(See Illus. 2-8.) Dividers, however, are used to measure length instead of diameter. They are used to "walk off" distances along the turning's axis as well as around its perimeter.

I keep the points on my dividers needle-sharp so that besides measuring, they will also score a fine scribe line when they touch the spinning blank. A fine scribed line is thinner than a pencil line and is, therefore, more accurate. This way, I can lay out a turning while the lathe is running.

You should also own several pairs of dividers of different lengths.

SIZING TOOLS

A special guide called a sizing tool is often used with the parting tool to lay out a turning. This tool is a curved arm that fits over the end of the parting tool. (See Illus. 2-9.) The other end of the sizing tool's arm projects in front of the parting tool's cutting edge. You can adjust the distance between the sizing tool's outer end and the cutting edge by moving the sizing tool forward and back on the parting tool's blade. In use, you score a groove with the parting tool and stop when the end of the sizing tool is able to slip over the bottom of the cut.

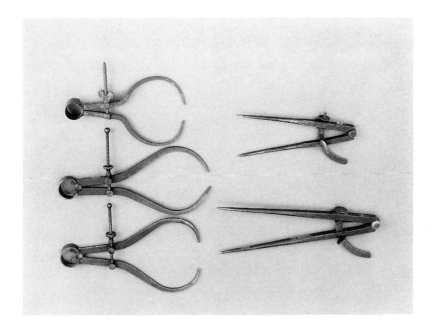

Illus. 2-8. Also needed when turning are tools that measure lengths and diameters. I own several pairs of calipers and dividers.

As long as you do not readjust the tool, it will make cuts of exactly the same depth. One disadvantage, however, is that it takes time to readjust the tool, so, therefore, a sizing tool is most efficient for special situations where it is necessary to make a series of the same detail. The sizing tool is discussed further in Chapter 7.

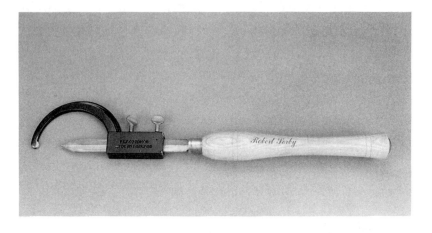

Illus. 2-9. A parting tool is sometimes used with a sizing tool, which can be moved back and forth to alter the distance between it and the cutting edge.

3

SHARPENING TECHNIQUES

As a woodworker, you have had to sharpen the tools that you use at the bench. Although, there are some similarities between sharpening lathe tools and other woodworking tools (particularly chisels), there are also some important differences. These differences are highlighted in this chapter.

Sharpening is not an arcane science. It is a skill and it is very easy to learn. However, too many woodworkers are overwhelmed and confused by the jargon of sharpening. They hear talk about cutting angles, clearance angles, etc., and become baffled. In fact, the most common questions I am asked are, "What angle do you sharpen to?" and "How often do you sharpen?" The answers to these questions will be discussed later.

Grinding

The first step in sharpening is to grind the cutting edge to the desired shape. For this job, I use a two-wheeled bench grinder. Sanding belts are very popular, but I find that they make the bezel longer than I like. Also, they make it very difficult to hollow-grind (see below).

The stone I use most often on my grinder is 100 grit (fine). If you, too, choose to use a bench grinder, keep the wheels running true by regularly dressing them. A diamond dresser works fine. A diamond dresser is a short metal rod with an industrial diamond set into one end (available at industrial supply houses).

Illus. 3-1. One way to keep the grinding wheels running true is with a diamond dresser. This tool also freshens the wheel's surface when it becomes clogged.

The dresser also freshens the surface of the wheel by exposing new abrasive particles. (See Illus. 3-1.) If the edge is kept free from clogging and glazing, the wheel will create less heat. However, you should still keep a container of water by the grinder and cool the tool often.

Whatever form of grinder you use, practice with it until you have the control necessary to create whatever shape cutting edge a tool requires. You should also be able to grind without causing so much heat that the steel turns blue and becomes too soft to hold a sharp edge.

A sharp edge is the result of two surfaces coming together at an angle. On most cutting tools (for example, a bench chisel), one side of the blade is flat. Although many woodworking magazines and authors refer to the sloping surface (the one that is ground) as a bevel, the more accurate word is bezel. To be more precise, the bezel on a chisel is called a "cannel," although in this book I will refer to it as a bezel.

Turning tools are different from most cutting tools used at the bench in that many do not have a flat surface opposite the bezel. Gouges have a concave surface opposite the bezel, but on many other turning tools (like skews and parting tools) the cutting edge is formed by the intersection of two bezels. The bezel on many cutting tools used on the bench (planes, chisels, etc.) should be at about 30 degrees. However, turning tools have different angles. Below I give the approximate angle of the bezels on my tools. Do not let these numbers make you nervous. You only have to approximate the angle. It is far more important that right now you are able to sharpen your turning tools so that you can learn to turn. Most times, I simply grind the tool so it does its job, and forget about its cutting angle.

One important concept to remember is that the heavier the work done by the tool, the steeper the angle of the bezel should be. This creates a stronger edge that is more capable of withstanding shock. Thus, a heavy roughing gouge will have a steeper angle than a spindle gouge that is used for shaping, which is more delicate work.

As noted above, I prefer to hollow-grind my tools, as a hollow grind creates a distinct edge and a heel. (An edge and heel have benefits that will be explained below.) This means that rather than being a true, flat surface, the bezel is slightly concave. If you are using a bench grinder, this shape occurs naturally, resulting from the circular shape of the wheel. (See Illus. 3-2.)

Your gouges will usually require more frequent grinding than any of your other turning tools. This is because the major amount of wood you remove when turning is cut with these tools, and, as a result, they become dull much more often.

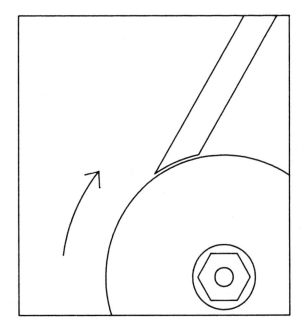

Illus. 3-2. The round edge of a grinding wheel creates a concave bezel which is said to be hollow-ground.

GRINDING ROUGHING GOUGES

Roughing gouges have a straight cutting edge—one that is at a right angle to the sides of the blade—just like that on a bench gouge. When you are grinding a roughing gouge, lay the center of the curved body on the tool rest with the handle held low. (See Illus. 3-3.) Raise the handle, bringing the center of the curved bezel into contact with the wheel. Then, grind

Illus. 3-3. When grinding a rough-ing gouge, lay the bottom of the curved blade on the tool rest with the handle held low.

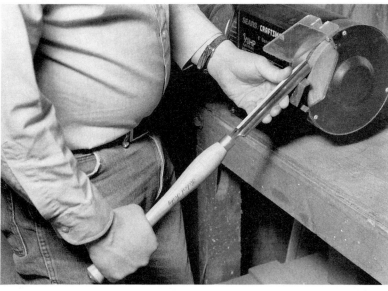

Illus. 3-4. Grind each side of the roughing gouge's edge by rolling the tool from side to side on its long axis.

each half of the edge by rolling the tool from side to side, rotating it on its long axis. (See Illus. 3-4.) With practice, you will be able to grind a cutting edge that is perfectly straight from one corner to the other.

A roughing gouge bezel should be ground to about 40–45 degrees.

GRINDING SPINDLE GOUGES

Spindle gouges have a convex curved edge, similar in shape to the end of your thumb. As noted in the last chapter, narrow gouges (¼- and ⅜-inch wide) are often called "lady finger" gouges, because their edges are usually more elliptical.

To grind a spindle gouge, first lay the gouge on the tool rest with the center of its edge in contact with the revolving stone. Because the cutting edge is rounded, you have to move the handle in two different directions simultaneously. First, twist the handle so that the gouge's body rolls on the rest. This is the same motion as used to grind a roughing gouge, and is described above. At the same time, swing the handle in a gentle arc, raising it slightly. (See Illus. 3-5.) This motion will keep the curved bezel in contact with the stone, while creating the correct shape.

Grind the other half of the bezel in the same way. Watch closely and you will see that throughout this process the far end of the tool's handle will move in a shallow arc. Again, with practice you will learn to grind an edge that is a smooth, symmetrical curve. Spindle gouges are sharpened to 35–40 degrees. Narrower spindle gouges have shallower angles.

GRINDING SKEWS

When grinding a skew, you should be concerned with the following: 1, that the cutting edge is centered on the end of the blade (Illus. 3-6A); 2, that the bezels are the same width on both sides of the blade (Illus. 3-6B); 3, that the bezels have a constant width along their entire length (Illus. 3-6B); and 4, that the cutting edge is skewed at about a 75-degree angle to the edges of the blade (Illus. 3-6C).

Before beginning, consider how you would go about grinding a bench chisel. The cutting edge of a bench chisel is at a right angle to the blade's sides, so you hold its handle in line with the wheel. You lower the end of the handle and slowly raise it to bring the bezel against the revolving stone. Then, you slide the handle and blade from side to side, maintaining the grinding angle and making certain that the tool is kept parallel to the wheel.

A skew is ground in the same way, except that the handle is held at about 75 degrees to

Illus. 3-5. Grind a spindle gouge by twisting the handle and simultaneously raising the handle through a gentle arc.

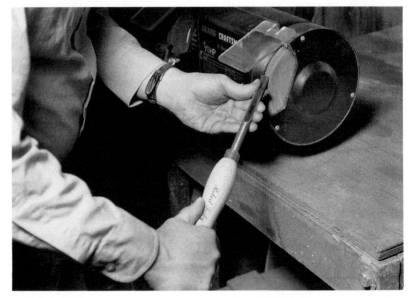

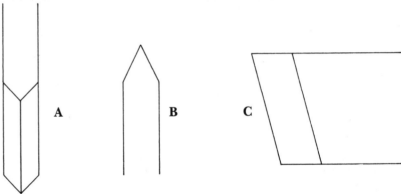

Illus. 3-6. When grinding a skew, make sure that: A) the cutting edge is centered on the blade B) the bezels are a constant width and the same width on both sides of the blade C) the cutting edge is about 75 degrees to the edges of the blade.

A   **B**   **C**

the revolving wheel. (See Illus. 3-7.) (Don't worry about getting this angle exact.) You must begin on one side or the other. Being right-handed, I naturally grind the left-hand bezel first. This means that I grip the handle with my right hand, and hold the tool on the rest with my left.

Place the skew on the rest with the handle low, and bring it into contact with the wheel by slowly raising the handle. Now, move the skew both to the right and to the left, being sure to hold it at 75 degrees to the wheel.

When one side is done, grind the other. Roll the tool over and, keeping the handle at 75 degrees, angle it in the opposite direction. (See Illus. 3-8.) Repeat the process. In my case, I would now be grinding the right-hand bezel. My left hand would be on the handle, while my right hand would be holding the skew against the rest.

As you grind this second bezel, check often to see that is the same width as the first. Together, the two bezels will form about a 45-degree angle. Thus, each should be ground at

Illus. 3-7. To grind a skew, hold the handle at about a 75-degree angle to the wheel. Slide the tool from side to side, as you would when grinding a bench chisel.

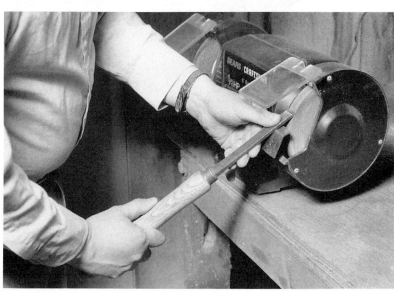

Illus. 3-8. Grind the skew's other bezel with the handle angled in the other direction.

about 22–23 degrees to the center of the blade.

As explored in Chapter 6, you can often use a skew to plane a turned surface smooth and to make what is called a rolling cut. These techniques require that the tool pivot on the blade's lower edge. These are important cuts, and the best results are obtained when they are made as smoothly as possible. However, the edge of a skew's blade is square, having two corners. This is hardly a surface that pivots easily.

Therefore, this edge should be rounded. First try to round the edge with a file. Often, however, the skew's blade is hardened, and the file will not cut. The rounding then has to be done on a grinder. Be careful not to overheat the blade, as this can soften it. Try to make the newly curved edge as uniform and regular as possible. When you test your skew, you will find that it rolls much more smoothly. (See Illus. 3-9).

GRINDING PARTING TOOLS

The parting tool I use has an unusual cross section, often called a diamond section. It is thickest along its centerline. This is an important factor to consider when grinding a parting tool.

Like the skew, parting tools have two bezels that meet to form the cutting edge. The cutting edge is horizontal and short, rather than vertical and tall. This is because the bezels meet on the narrow dimension rather than the long one. In other words, while the skew's cutting

edge is used nearly vertical to the rest, the parting tool's is parallel to the rest.

When you grind a parting tool, its cutting edge must align with the rib running down both sides of the tool's blade. This is important because when a parting tool is ground correctly, its cutting edge is located at the widest point, and the widths of the two bezels taper away with the more narrow sides. Thus, when the tool makes a parting cut—a narrow, deep groove—only the corners of the cutting edge are in contact with the groove's sides. This reduces the possibility of binding, or damage (such as burning) due to friction.

Grind the parting tool as you would a bench chisel, with the only difference that the blade is held on its edge rather than on its side. The cutting edge is square to the sides, so hold the handle in line with the rotation of the grinding wheel. (See Illus. 3-10.)

Grind one side first. Since the blade is so narrow, no side-to-side movement across the wheel is necessary. In fact, the only motion you make is to raise the handle slightly to keep the bezel against the wheel. Because you are not moving it from side to side, you do have to be careful that the tool does not overheat and loose its temper. This will result in a soft spot that will not hold an edge.

When the first bezel is complete, turn the tool over and grind the second bezel the same way. Make sure that its cutting edge stays on the raised center rib.

Illus. 3-9. If you round the bottom edge of the skew, it will roll more smoothly.

Illus. 3-10. Grind a parting tool as you would a bench chisel. The handle should be held in line with the rotation of the wheel.

GRINDING DIAMOND POINTS

Diamond points also have two bezels. These bezels, however, are on the same side of the blade. When you look at them they resemble the facets of a diamond. The two bezels, set at an angle to each other, result in two cutting edges. The blade's pointed end is actually the result of their intersection. The smaller the angle of intersection, the more pointed the tool. The two cutting edges on my diamond point intersect to form a 110 degree angle. Each edge is about 145 degrees to the sides of the tool.

When grinding a diamond point, think of each cutting edge as a small skew. Place the tool against the wheel and grind it as you would a skew, moving the cutting edge back and forth while holding the handle at the correct angle relative to the wheel. (See Illus. 3-11.) A right-hander would naturally start grinding the tool by holding the handle in his right hand. His left hand would press the blade against the wheel. This position allows him to grind the right-hand bezel.

When finished with one bezel, do not invert the tool as you would a skew. Simply change

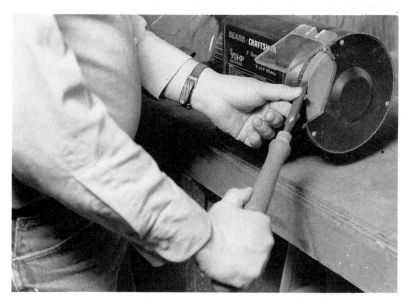

Illus. 3-11. Grind each side of the diamond point as you would the sides of a small skew. Move the edge back and forth without changing the handle's angle.

hands, and you will be in position to grind the second side. If you had taken a picture of your position when grinding the first edge, it would be a mirror image of your position when grinding the second edge. (See Illus. 3-12.)

When sharpening the diamond point, practice so that the ridge created by the two intersecting bezels is parallel to the tool's sides.

Honing

WHETSTONES

Grinding only shapes the cutting edge and bezel. It does not create a sharp edge that will cut wood easily and cleanly. A sharp edge can only be created by honing. For this step, whetstones are needed. You should own at the very least a medium- and fine-grade stone.

It really does not matter what type of whetstone you use. Japanese water stones, however, are currently popular with woodworkers. They are inexpensive and come in a variety of grits. One disadvantage is that they have to be kept wet. This requires that you store them in a tub of water. If any water splashes about when you are using the stones, it will spot and rust other tools. So, if you choose to own water stones you also have to create a separate sharpening station.

Another disadvantage is that water stones are soft and wear quickly. Since turning tools are narrow (unlike plane blades), they can quickly wear a trough in a water stone. Fortunately, water stones can be easily flattened. Do this on a sheet of plate glass to which you have adhered 400 or 320 wet or dry sandpaper (silicon carbide).

Oilstones, both natural and man-made, are the more traditional alternative. They tend to be more expensive than water stones, but are usually more durable. Still, over time a trough will wear in them, too. When you are honing an oilstone, you will have to lubricate it with oil. The oil leaves a dirty film on your fingers. This oily film gets on everything you touch, even if you wipe your hands when done.

Use man-made ceramic stones. They are very hard, and seem to retain their flatness. I have not noticed the slightest hint of a trough in either of mine after six years of use. Also, ceramic stones are used dry. This is certainly more convenient.

When the surface of a ceramic stone becomes glazed with metal dust, it can be quickly cleaned with a sponge and bathroom scouring powder. Let the stone dry thoroughly before using it again. It will only take a few minutes to dry.

SLIPSTONES

Whetstones are fine for honing most lathe tools. Even though gouge bezels are curved, they can still be honed on a flat surface. Simply

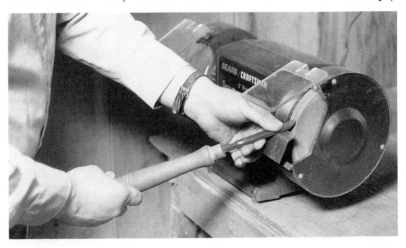

Illus. 3-12. To grind the diamond point's other bezel, do not turn the tool over, as you would with a skew. Simply change hands and angle the handle the other way.

roll the bezel as you hone. The insides of gouges, however, have to be honed with slipstones. Most slipstones have a cross section that looks like an elongated tear drop. They have two flat sides with two round edges: one wide, the other narrow. The ends are flat with square corners. (See Illus. 3-13.)

Slipstones are made of the same natural and man-made materials as whetstones. The Japanese also make water-lubricated slipstones. All come in the same grades as whetstones.

FILES

Files (sometimes called "gun files") are long, narrow stones that come in special shapes. They are useful in many sharpening jobs. Following are some of the cross sections files can have: triangular, round, teardrop, square, and knife edge.

Files are usually made of man-made materials. Mine are made of the same ceramic materials as my whetstones. I use round- and teardrop-shaped files most often on lathe tools. (See Illus. 3-14.)

HONING PROCEDURE

Honing is done the same way, no matter what type of whetstone is used. Remember, an edge

Illus. 3-13. A group of slipstones. The different colors represent different degrees of fineness. Note that the slipstones taper in thickness and have round edges that make them handy for honing gouges.

Illus. 3-14. A group of ceramic files with various cross sections. From left to right, they are as follow: a round file, a triangular file, a teardrop file, and a square file.

is the result of two surfaces meeting at an angle. Only when the two intersecting surfaces are polished so smooth they have a mirror surface can there be a condition called "sharp." Sharp means that the edge is keen enough to slice cleanly through wood.

Hold the bevel of a recently ground tool up to the light, and look carefully. You'll note that the grinding wheel's abrasive particles have roughly scratched the surface. (See Illus. 3-15.) These scratches are even more pronounced under a magnifying glass. Where the scratches meet the edge, they produce serrations like the teeth on a saw. This ragged edge is deceptive, for it will cut easily (although not cleanly) for a very short while. This is because, in effect, the edge is a tiny saw. However, it quickly becomes worn and very dull. If you were to rely on this type of edge you would have to constantly regrind it on a grinding wheel. You would not only waste a lot of time grinding (it takes a lot longer than honing), you would quickly squander your tool's steel.

The process of honing removes these heavy scratches by making scratches that are increasingly finer and finer. Eventually, these scratches become too microscopic to be seen, and the metal takes on a mirror-like polish. However, it is critical that both intersecting surfaces be polished. If you were to concentrate on only one, the scratches on the other would always result in a ragged edge.

If your tool has a flat side (for example, a diamond point), lay that side on the stone and polish it. Hold the blade perfectly flat on the stone. Never raise it even slightly, as this will round the cutting edge. Move the tool in whichever pattern you prefer: figure eight, circles, back-and-forth, or side-to-side. Periodic inspections will tell you how well the polish is developing. The entire surface does not have to be polished, only the area along the cutting edge. Look very closely to be sure that the polish extends right out to the very edge.

Start this process with a medium stone, and follow with a fine stone. The result should be a mirror polish, one that is so smooth you can see yourself in its reflection. Anything less will not produce a razor-sharp edge.

When sharpening a gouge, you first have to hone the inside surface, just behind the cutting edge. (See Illus. 3-16.) This has to be done with a slipstone. Hold the slipstone perfectly flat against the steel. If you allow it to rock, it will round the edge. (See Illus. 3-17.)

Because the surface is concave, you will be limited in what patterns you can use. On a narrow "lady finger" gouge, all you can basically do is move the slipstone back and forth. On a large gouge, you may be able to make circles or

Illus. 3-15. A grinding wheel will leave coarse scratches on a bezel. These scratches produce microscopic serrations on the cutting edge, much like the teeth on a tiny saw. Although this ragged edge will cut easily, it will not cut cleanly, and it quickly dulls.

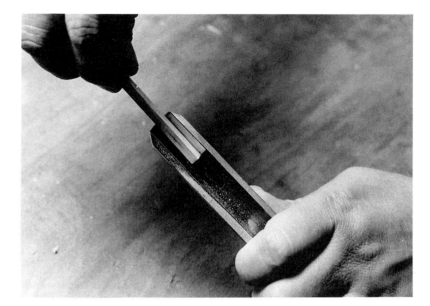

Illus. 3-16. Use a slipstone to polish the inside surface of both roughing and spindle gouges.

a figure 8. Honing this surface is a slow process and it takes patience. However, the results will be worthwhile.

After honing the flat side of a tool (if it has one), the next step is to hone the tool's bezel(s). In this step, it is important that the tool does not rock on its bezel. If you hold the tool too low, you will be honing the heel. (See Illus. 3-17.) If you hold the tool too high, you will round the cutting edge. To keep the tool from rocking hollow-grind the bezel so that it has a distinct edge and heel. To do this, first set the heel of the bezel on the stone. This angle is, of course, too low to hone. Slowly raise the handle until the cutting edge is also touching the stone's surface. The bezel is now in contact at

two points: the heel and the edge. If you are careful to hold it in this position while honing, you will not inadvertently round the edge.

With both the heel and edge in contact with the stone, move it in the pattern you prefer. Take the tool off the stone after a dozen or more passes. You should see a narrow line of polish on the heel and at the cutting edge. (See Illus. 3-18.) As long as both edges are being polished uniformly, the edge is not becoming round. Because you are only honing these two narrow surfaces, honing a hollow-ground bezel is very quick and easy to do. (See Illus. 3-19.)

By honing, you have made a very narrow flat surface at the cutting edge of the hollow-ground bezel. This polished flat surface meets

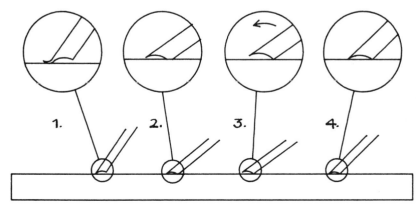

1.   2.   3.   4.

Illus. 3-17. If you hold the tool too high when honing, you will roll the edge as shown in 1. If the tool is too low, the honing only takes place on the heel, as shown in 2. To locate the correct angle, place the heel on the stone as shown in 3 and raise the back end until the edge comes in contact with the stone, as shown in 4. Make sure that both surfaces stay in contact with the stone while you are honing.

Illus. 3-18. You do not have to hone the entire surface of a hollow-ground bezel, only a narrow strip along the cutting edge. Note that the bezel's heel is also honed.

Illus. 3-19. 1 shows a hollow-ground edge. Honing creates narrow, flat surfaces on the heel and edge, as shown in 2. Each honing removes metal from these surfaces, increasing their widths. Eventually, these two surfaces will merge, as shown in 3. When this happens, it is time to re-grind. If you do not, and instead continue to hone, you have to re-move metal from the entire width of the bezel. This is a lot more work.

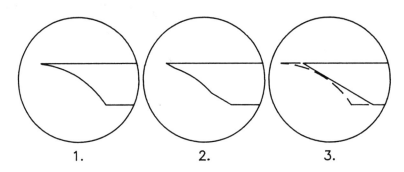

1.   2.   3.

at an angle with the perfectly flat and polished opposite side, and creates the condition called "sharp."

If you are sharpening a diamond point, hone each of the angled cutting edges separately. If you are sharpening a tool that has two bezels that intersect, such as a skew or parting tool, "sharp" will not occur until you have honed both bezels. Hone both bezels as just described. (See Illus. 3-20.)

Honing a gouge is slightly more difficult. Some woodworkers prefer to hold the gouge and work the stone over the bezel. I only do this on every large roughing gouges. For spindle gouges, I prefer to place the stone on the bench and move the tool. This gives me better control.

When honing a gouge's bezel, move the tool in whatever pattern you prefer. However, slowly rotate the blade so that the entire length of the edge is for awhile in contact with the stone. Remember to keep both the heel and edge touching. When you think you are done, exam-ine the bezel in bright light. You should be able to see the sheen that has developed during the

honing process. The sheen should be uniform along the entire bezel, and should continue right out to the edge. (See Illus. 3-21.)

If the gouge is too long (or too big) to run over the stone, you will have to hold the stone and run it over the tool's edge. (See Illus. 3-22.) Normally, the only gouge I have to do this to is my 1¼-inch roughing gouge. Hold the gouge on the bench or against your stomach and hone the bezel with a slipstone. Make sure that you first place the stone in contact with the heel, and then roll it until it also touches the cutting edge. Be sure not to accidentally brush your hand against the edge.

Work the slipstone over the entire length of the bezel. You can use any stroke you like: cir-cle, figure eight, side-to-side, or back-and-forth. Be sure that the slipstone rides on the heel as well as the edge. Examine the bezel closely to be sure that you have polished right out to the edge.

Check the polish along the bezel. It should extend along the entire length of the edge and should be brought to a mirror-like finish.

Illus. 3-20. Hone each of a diamond point's bezels as you would one side of a skew.

Illus. 3-21. When honing a gouge, make sure to slowly rotate the handle so that the entire edge is polished.

Stropping

After you have honed the bezel, the edge of the blade should be sharp. Test its sharpness with the tip of your thumb. If your skin is snagged by a slight wire edge, strop this edge away. Stropping can be done on a buffing wheel impregnated with an abrasive compound. I use grey steel, but jeweler's rouge (which is more fine) will also work. (See Illus. 3-23.) Simply touch the edge momentarily against the wheel. Any longer, and you risk rounding the edge.

Next, with a bright light shining over your shoulder, hold the blade so you are looking directly at its edge. If it is sharp, it will not be visible in this inspection. If you see even the narrowest sliver of surface glinting in the light, your tool is not sharp in that location.

Illus. 3-22 (left). Sometimes it is easier to hone a large gouge by running the stone over its bezel, rather than the other way around.

Illus. 3-23. Impregnate your buffing wheel with a buffing compound such as grey steel.

Determining When to Sharpen a Tool

As you use a tool, the cutting action creates friction which, in time, blunts the edge. Therefore, how often you sharpen a tool depends on how much you have used it, not the amount of time that has elapsed since you last sharpened it. It is time to resharpen the tool (usually by re-honing) when the tool no longer cuts easily and cleanly.

The polished surface along the edge of a hollow-ground bezel becomes wider with each honing. (See Illus. 3-18.) So does the surface on the heel. Eventually, the two surfaces will merge so that when honing you are polishing the entire bezel. This requires a lot more time and effort. It also creates more wear on your stones. When the two surfaces have merged, it is time to grind a new hollow-ground bezel.

Sharpening Procedure for the Lathe

So far all the sharpening procedures explored involved turning tools. There are also sharpening-related jobs that have to be done to the lathe. The spurs on the drive center must bite easily and firmly into the end of the blank. They cannot do this if they are dull, rounded, or battered. You should sharpen them when you first acquire your lathe, and periodically maintain them.

To sharpen the spurs, first knock the drive center out of the headstock spindle by inserting a drift through its back end. Rap the drift with a hammer, and catch the drive center with your free hand.

The center is so hard, a file will just skate across the spurs, and, as a result, you will have to grind them. Each spur is very much like a tiny chisel. It has a flat surface and, opposite that, a bezel ground at about 35 degrees. (See Illus. 3-24.)

Do as little grinding as is necessary to restore the bezel, as the spur is already quite short. Also, you do not want to create any heat. Heat will soften the hard spurs. If the edge of the bezel is still ragged even after you have ground the bezel, you may have to touch up the flat side of the spurs. Do this on the flat side of your stone, rather than on its round edge.

While you are grinding the spurs, purposely make a notch in the end of one of them. This particular spur will then make an imprint in the end of the blank that can be easily distinguished. (See Illus. 3-25.) Should you have to remove a partially completed turning from the lathe, or should you later have to work again on a completed turning, it is helpful to know ex-

Illus. 3-24. The spurs on a drive center should be kept sharp. Occasionally, they need to be ground. Their bezels are at about 35 degrees. Be careful to not create any heat, as this could soften the hard steel.

Illus. 3-25. Make a notch in one of the spurs. This creates an easily distinguished imprint which allows you to always return a piece of wood to the same position.

actly how it was originally mounted. Every spur is slightly different, and if the turning is not put back exactly as it was, it can be slightly eccentric. Make the notch on the grinding wheel's sharp corner.

The point on the drive center should also be sharp. If it is dull or round, it, too, should be reground. The point is usually removable. It is held in place by an Allen screw. If you loosen the Allen screw, you can draw the point out of the drive center.

Sharpen the point on the grindstone. Hold the point in your fingertips and slowly revolve it so that the end's entire circumference is ground to a uniform taper. This way, the point will bite easily and cleanly into the blank, staying exactly on the intersection of the X that locates the blank's centerline. (See Chapter 6.)

When you return the point to the drive center, adjust it so that it stands just slightly above the ends of the spurs. This way, it engages the wood in advance of the spurs, making it easier for you to center the blank when chucking it up in the lathe.

You will learn in Chapter 5 that in order for you to make many shaping cuts, the tool has to move smoothly over the rest. This cannot happen if the rest's bearing surface is rough. Roughness is not necessarily the result of damage. The factory may have only rough-ground the surface, or did not grind it at all, leaving it just as it was cast. To smooth the bearing surface, first run a file over it. A file will cut most quickly if it is held at a slight angle, in a technique called draw filing. (See Illus. 3-26.) Next, smooth the surface with either sandpaper or emery cloth. Depending on the humidity, the newly exposed metal may eventually develop a thin layer of rust. This, too, can impede the fluid movement of the tools. You can quickly remove the rust by buffing it with a fine (200-grit) sandpaper.

Illus. 3-26. Draw-filing the top of your rest will remove any imperfections that might interfere with the smooth movement of your tools. Finish with sandpaper or emery cloth.

4
SAFETY

Because the lathe only spins the blank and does not actually cut it, many turners think of it as a tool rather than a machine. When it comes to safety, however, the lathe should be thought of as a machine. And although it is one of the least dangerous machines used by wood-workers, you do have to observe certain precautions when using a lathe.

The most common injury experienced by woodturners is pinched skin, usually caught between the blank and the rest. This can give you a blood blister, a bruise, and even a friction burn. However, the potential for worse injuries does exist. In rare occasions, serious injuries have occurred.

Though many turners do not wear eye or face protection while using the lathe, a full face shield is strongly recommended. (See Illus. 4-1.) A pair of goggles will protect your eyes, but the shield covers your entire face and neck. All that remains exposed is the top of your forehead above the hairline. I keep my shield hanging on a hook above the lathe, and do not turn on the machine until I am wearing it.

The clear plastic visor on the shield is soft and flexible so that it will not shatter if struck, but it will scratch if cleaned regularly. Eventually it becomes covered with so many fine scratches that it becomes difficult to see through. For this reason, it is recommended that you purchase face shields with plastic visors that can be replaced. These shields have one disadvantage that can be potentially dangerous: you exhale onto the inside surface of the visor, just below your eyes. If the plastic is cooler than your breath, condensation will form on the inside, obscuring your vision. This problem occurs most often in the winter. To

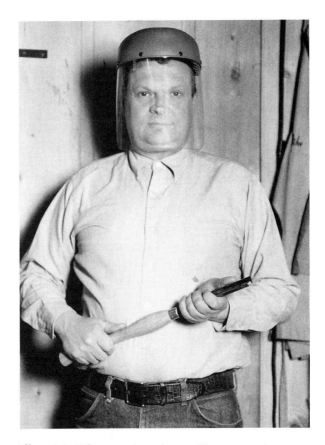

Illus. 4-1. When turning, dress safely. Wear a face shield, remove any jewelry, and button your sleeves. To keep out chips, wear a cotton shirt, button the collar, and tuck in your shirttails. Also wear sturdy shoes and long pants.

prevent this condensation, warm the visor before putting on the shield. You can warm the visor by holding it above the stove for a minute or by running it under warm water.

Never wear loose-fitting clothes when working on a lathe. Button your shirt cuffs. Also button your collar to keep out stray chips. If they get inside your shirt, they will work their way down your chest, eventually gathering around the belt line. This can be very annoying.

If your work shirts have flaps over their pockets, make sure they are closed. Otherwise you can end up with pockets full of shavings.

Avoid wearing pants with cuffs, as these, too, collect volumes of chips. Also try to avoid wearing clothes that have a fuzzy surface, such as sweatshirts, sweaters or chamois shirts, because the dust and chips stick to them.

It is advisable to wear long sleeve shirts when turning, because the heavy chips made when roughing a billet round can slap against your wrist. This can be painful. Also, if you are allergic to some species of woods, make sure that your arms or other parts of your body are protected.

When installing your lathe, be sure to mount it in a place where the floor is solid. This will prevent it from "walking" due to vibration. A concrete floor is good. Although you can get sore feet standing on it, the lathe will not move. (Before turning, I soften my concrete floor by pushing together a mat of chips and standing on that.)

Keep the space around the lathe clear so that your body and arms are not crowded while you are woodturning. Clean up the shavings when you are done, as they present a fire hazard. (My wife uses those I make as garden mulch.) When sweeping them, watch closely for any tools that may have accidentally fallen in them.

The area around the lathe (and especially the space between the head and tail stock) should be well-lighted. I have hung a fluorescent tube ceiling light directly over mine.

Mount the Off/On switch where you can reach it easily and quickly in an emergency. Mine is on my left side, just below my hip. A toggle-type switch is a good choice because you can shut it off with a brush of your hand.

Keep your tools in a rack where they can be easily reached. My rack is attached to the lathe base and is placed to my right at about hip level. It is unwise to hang your tools behind your lathe so that you have to reach over the spinning blank.

It is best to return the tools to the rack as you use them, though I have to admit I very seldom do this. When woodturning, I too often lay a tool on the lathe bed, especially if I will need it again in a short while. Every now and then the tool will fall (usually on its cutting edge). Knowing this, I always wear heavy shoes, never sandals or sneakers.

Before changing speeds or working on the V-belt, unplug the machine. When done, always replace your pulley cover. Before starting the motor, tap the cover to make sure that it has not become loose due to vibration.

Before turning the lathe on, always spin the blank by hand to make sure that it will clear the rest. Although most turners do not shut off their lathe when moving the rest, do so if the locking levers on your machine are in awkward places.

Before doing any carving, indexing, or any other operations where the lathe is used as a clamping or holding tool (see Chapters 12 and 13), be sure to unplug the machine to ensure against accidentally starting it.

Also, be careful when handling or carrying your lathe tools. They are like short spears, and are equally dangerous. When walking with them, point their blades towards the floor to protect yourself should you stumble. Be extra cautious if you are working around other people.

5

TURNING BLANKS

This chapter and Chapters 6 and 7 should be read together. Here I describe how turning tools are used to rough-round blanks and reduce them to diameter. The next two chapters explain how to identify those shapes or elements that can be cut with turning tools, and describe the actual shaping techniques. These procedures are all part of the turning process.

There is one important point to consider before reading on: In woodturning, there are many ways to make the same cut. The procedures I am about to describe are very successful. But they are not the only procedures that can be used. You may decide to adapt your own technique. As long as you have successful results with it, continue to use it.

Nothing creates more problems for a new turner than learning to make the tools cut cleanly. When cut properly, a piece turned by hand will need little or no sanding. The tools will leave the wood quite smooth. So if you find yourself doing a lot of sanding, take some time to reconsider your cutting technique.

The piece will be cut correctly only if you hold and manipulate the tool correctly and use the correct cutting angle (see below and Chapter 6)—the angle at which the tool most efficiently slices a chip from the blank. When you are doing both properly, the shavings should come off the spinning blank in solid pieces. If you are creating a lot of dust, you are scraping and not cutting, and the surface you make will be rough and tattered.

Scraping not only mars the wood, it is also hard on the tools. It creates a lot of friction, which results in heat and wear. While working at the bench, you have become familiar with the cutting tools you use to make furniture and architectural elements. For example, you know that when you use a hand plane on a board, it cuts thin, even shavings and leaves behind a glassy smooth surface that no sandpaper can create. A keen edge on a plane blade will eventually become dull, but properly sharpened it will cut cleanly for a long time.

Now, imagine taking the blade out of the plane and using it as a scraper. You would have to hold it at a high angle, so that it was standing right up on the cutting edge. You would be able to remove a shaving by scraping this way, but the friction you create will soon dull the edge.

The same thing happens to lathe tools if the edge is engaging the spinning wood at too high an angle. The tool scrapes rather than cuts. Below I discuss how to properly cut with a lathe tool.

Proper Cutting Techniques

No matter what tool you use to cut, you should always be aware of grain direction. Your experience at the bench has taught you that pushing a tool such as a plane into rising grain will not result in as clean a cut as can be obtained working in the other direction. The same is true in turning. When you remove wood, you cut through layers of annual growth and expose end grain. (See Illus. 5-1.) Therefore, you always have to continue to cut in the same direction. The phrase used to describe this action

Illus. 5-1. Whenever you make an element, make sure to always cut "downhill" so that you do not cut against the grain. Ignoring this will result in a rough surface. Furthermore, when you are making some details, such as a cove, the end grain can grab a tool and pull it out of control.

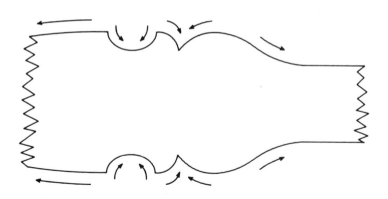

is "cutting downhill." When you cut uphill, you cut against the grain and leave a more ragged cut. Understanding these techniques is particularly important when you are making finishing cuts such as when planing (see below).

CUTTING WITH A GOUGE

Most of the cutting done with a gouge (whether deep or standard flute, or roughing or spindle) occurs on the sides of the cutting edge, rather than in the middle. This means that much of the time the gouge is used on the sides of its curved blade, rather than resting on the bottom of the arc.

Do the following to find the cutting angle: Round a blank (see Chapter 6). While it spins, lay the tool's bezel on the wood, holding the tool at about a 65-degree angle to the axis of the blank (the handle is angled away from you). (See Illus. 5-2.) This is a comfortable position for anyone who has ever pushed a bench plane, for, as you know, a plane cuts best if held slightly askew.

The gouge cannot cut with its bezel riding on the blank because its edge cannot engage the wood. The edge is too high. The optimum cutting angle will be lower. Using the hand with which you hold the tool handle (for right-handed people, the right hand), slowly begin to draw the handle rearwards, all the time keeping the bezel on the blank. You are only

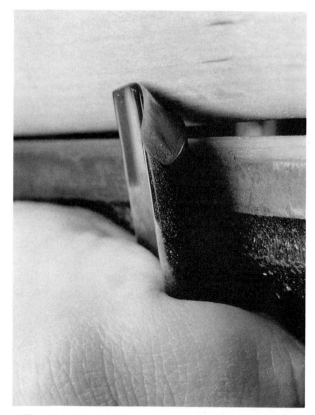

Illus. 5-2. To find the cutting angle, lay the gouge's bezel on the spinning blank, holding the handle at about 65 degrees to the rest. Roll the gouge so that the blade's round bottom is turned away from you. Slowly pull the handle rearwards a fraction of an inch. This will lower the cutting edge into the wood.

going to move the edge a fraction of an inch. This motion will bring it into contact with the wood, and it will cut a shaving. Because you are not moving the tool sidewards, the cut will be very short. Also, the heel of the bezel should still be riding on the blank.

While the tool is in this position, only the very bottom of the curved cutting edge is in a position to cut. Now, roll the gouge towards the left (counterclockwise), so that the blade's round bottom is turned away from you at about 4 o'clock. This brings the left side of the curved cutting edge into contact with the wood. The tool handle should be directed away from you at about 65 degrees to the blank's axis. Meanwhile, the bezel should still be pressed against the wood. Doing this ensures that you have not raised the tool too high, approaching a scraping angle. Pull the gouge towards you. As long as the tool is in motion, it will peel off a shaving. (See Illus. 5-3.)

At the end of the cut, turn the gouge clockwise so it is rolling on the blade's right side. At the same time, pull the handle towards you so that it's angled at about 65 degrees to the blank's axis. Push the gouge away from you, and it will cut another shaving. Keep the bezel rubbing on the blank.

This is the basic cut made with both the roughing and spindle gouges. I will describe some other techniques in Chapters 6 and 7 when explaining how to rough-round and cut concave elements such as a cove.

CUTTING WITH A PARTING TOOL

The parting tool cuts differently than a gouge. Because it makes straight plunge cuts, it is held at 90 degrees to the wood rather than at an angle.

To find the cutting angle of a parting tool,

Illus. 5-3. Holding the cutting angle, pull the gouge towards you. It will cut a shaving, which will break up into little pieces. When you reach the end of the rest, roll the tool in the other direction, repeating the process for finding the cutting angle. Now, push the tool along the rest, and it will once again cut a shaving.

Illus. 5-4. To find the cutting angle for a parting tool, hold it at a right angle to the rest—the bezel riding on the wood. Pull the handle rearwards until the cutting edge engages. Lift the handle and push forward slowly. The tool will cut a straight-sided groove.

hold the lower bezel against the spinning wood. (See Illus. 5-4.) Slowly pull rearward on the handle, keeping the bezel in contact with the wood. This will lower the cutting edge, and it will soon begin to engage the wood. When it does, it will quickly cut a shallow groove. To make this groove even deeper, raise the back of the handle so that the tool pivots on the tool rest, and push forward at the same time. The shaving should come off in one long ribbon. However, because the shaving is being cut across the grain, it will break up very easily.

As will be explained in Chapters 6 and 7, the parting tool is used for sizing and laying out some of the elements that are used in spindle turning. However, it is also used for parting, which is a quick and efficient way of cutting turnings out of the lathe. Often, waste is left on each end of the turning where the centers make contact. This waste is later cut off with a saw. However, if you use a parting tool, you cut the turning out of the lathe while it is still running. This technique was often used by old-time production turners, who increased their efficiency by never shutting off the machine. They simply cut out the finished part and mounted a new blank while the lathe kept spinning.

To part a turning out of the lathe, make a parting cut until the remaining section is so thin (usually about the thickness of a match stick) that it snaps. The part will not fly out of the machine. Instead, it will fall gently onto the bed. Sometimes, small turnings are made two at a time; parting them out of the lathe separates them, saving the time necessary to saw them apart. (See Chapter 16.)

CUTTING WITH A SKEW

The skew is one of the most versatile tools you will use in turning. However, it is also the most difficult to master. Since you can do so much with a skew, it is worthwhile to practice and become proficient with it. Below are descriptions of the various cuts made with this tool.

Plunge Cuts

You have already learned how to use a parting tool. A skew can make very similar cuts. However, instead of making a groove, the skew is usually used to make plunge cuts with one open side. As a woodworker, you are familiar with rabbets, which are stepped edges on a board. Think of the skew as the tool you use for making rabbets in a spinning blank.

Consider the cutting technique used to make a square shoulder on a billet with a skew. First, use the heel of the skew to score a line where you want the shoulder to begin. This step is not essential, but it does eliminate any fuzz on the corner of the shoulder.

Next, place the skew in the same position as you would a parting tool.

However, in order for the bezel to be riding on the wood, place the blade on its side rather than its edge. Use the correct bezel—the one that allows you to use the skew's pointed toe. In Illus. 5-5, I am cutting a rabbet on the right-hand side of the turning; therefore the left bezel is riding on the wood, with the point aligned with the scored mark. It is also important that the cutting edge be parallel with the axis of the wood. This means that the handle will be angled to the right.

Now, pull the handle rearwards, lowering the cutting edge so that it engages the wood. Raise the rear end of the handle so that it pivots on the tool rest; at the same time, push forward slowly. This motion is the same one you would make with a parting tool. The skew will remove similar shavings, although they will be wider. Stop the cutting action when you reach the desired depth.

This same type of cut can be used in dozens of places on all types of turnings. One of the most common techniques is to make the fillets that separate the different elements in a turning. As you become more experienced as a turner, you will find more opportunities to use this cut in your own work.

Illus. 5-5. To make a square shoulder with a skew, lay the blade on its wide side with its toe pointing into the corner. The handle should be angled so that the cutting edge is parallel to the wood's axis (the lathe centers). Ride the bezel on the wood and slowly pull the handle rearwards, as you did with the parting tool. When the tool starts to cut, push it forward. Stop cutting when you have reached the desired depth.

Facing Off

If you make a plunge cut with either a parting tool or skew, the end grain in the cut's shoulder(s) will be left ragged. To make this surface as smooth as glass, you will have to face it. This technique can be done with either a skew or a diamond point (see below).

Rest the skew on its lower edge so that the heel does the cutting. Angle the handle away from the blank's axis so that the adjacent bezel is at very near a right angle to the axis and parallel to the shoulder: in other words, so that the bezel will ride on the wood's shoulder as it is being faced-off.

Slowly pull rearwards on the handle and pivot the blade on the rest so that it engages the wood. The heel will begin to score the wood and to shear a thin shaving off the shoulder. (See Illus. 5-6.) Pull up slowly on the end of the handle and, at the same time, push it slowly forward into the wood. The chip that is severed from the shoulder should be thin and disc-like, and the shoulder itself should gleam like glass. (See Illus. 5-7.)

Rolled Cuts

A rolled cut is very similar to a face-off cut. It will create the same glassy surface, and is used to shape round elements. (See Chapter 7.)

Illus. 5-6. To face off with a skew, hold the tool with the blade vertical. The handle is angled so that the nearest bezel is close to (but not perfectly) parallel to the shoulder. Slowly lift the handle, pushing the heel into the wood. Now, advance the skew. It will shear a thin, disc-like shaving.

Illus. 5-7. The faced-off shoulder will be so smooth that it gleams like glass.

To make a rolled cut, first make a scored line with the heel of the skew. This should also mark the deepest point of the cut (which is often the end of an element, such as the bottom of a vase). Move slightly to the right of the line and lay the skew on its side, with the bezel on that side riding on the turning. Roll the handle just slightly. This will lift the toe, and the heel will begin to engage the wood, lifting a shaving.

While rolling the tool with one hand, use your hand on the blade to pull the tool towards the scored line. At the same time, push the heel into the wood. (See Illus. 5-8.) The effect is a rolling action that causes the heel of the tool to travel along a curve. As it does, the blade will slice a chip and leave behind a curved surface.

If the curve needs to be longer than you can make with just a single cut, make a second cut that starts just to the right of the first. (See Illus. 5-9.) Repeat the motion, removing a second chip. Do this as many times as required to make the curve you wish. Start each cut slightly farther away from the starting point than the previous one.

Be careful when making this cut. If the skew's blade becomes too vertical, the heel will catch in the end grain and be dragged up the turning. When you shut off the lathe, you will find that the heel has made a deep spiral cut, perhaps ruining the piece.

To avoid this problem, make sure as you make each rolled cut that the lower bezel stays in contact with the curved surface it is cutting.

Illus. 5-8. To make a rolled cut, score a line. Then move slightly to the right and lay the skew on the right side of its wide blade, with the bezel riding on the spinning blank. Roll the blade by turning the handle; in this case, it is being turned counterclockwise. The heel will engage. Completing this rolling action will cause the edge to travel along a curve. If you keep the bezel riding on the wood, it will not be pulled out of control, and will leave a gleaming, round surface.

Illus. 5-9. If the detail needs a longer radius than you can cut in one pass, make a second cut, repeating the same motions. However, begin the second cut slightly farther right than the first. Keep the bezel riding on the wood.

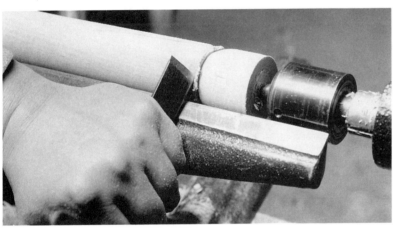

Illus. 5-10. To make a rolled cut in the opposite direction, lay the blade on its other side, slightly to the left of the scored line. Repeat the rolling action, but this time turn the handle clockwise.

As long as the bezel is riding on this surface, the angle is low enough that the tool will not get caught and pulled out of control. At this angle, the skew will cut a glassy, smooth surface.

In Illus. 5-8 and 5-9, I am cutting from right to left and drawing the tool towards me by turning it counterclockwise. You can also cut from left to right. The techniques are the same, but in the latter case you push the skew away from you by turning it clockwise. (See Illus. 5-10.)

Planing

Planing is one of the most difficult techniques to learn, but once you have mastered it you can produce surfaces on a turning that are nearly as smooth as the surface of a hand-planed board. Planing with a lathe eliminates the need for most sanding, and, because it can be done so quickly, it is the most efficient method for finishing your work. Also, it does not leave scratches that later become visible under the finish. (See Chapter 7.)

The size of the skew you will use to plane a turning is determined by the diameter of the blank and the size of the element being planed. I use a ¾-inch skew for large turnings, and a ½-inch skew for smaller ones.

When you plane a turning, you use the skew's sharp, straight-cutting edge to smooth the turning. To learn this technique, first turn a cylinder that is thick enough to withstand vibration. (See Chapter 6.) The surface of the cylinder will have ripples that were produced by the gouge. Planing will remove these tool marks.

To plane the cylinder with a skew place the skew on the tool rest, at the right end of the blank. The heel should face the direction of travel, which in this case is from right to left. The cutting edge should be angled (skewed) away from you at about 65 degrees to the wood's axis in the same way you would hold a gouge. (See Illus. 5-11.)

The right-hand bezel should be resting on the spinning wood. Only about the lower two-thirds of the bezel should be in actual contact with the blank. The heel will not be cutting. The nose *must* be elevated above the wood. Slowly raise the handle and twist it ever so slightly towards your body. This will engage the cutting edge with the wood. Make sure that the lower bezel is still rubbing on the blank's surface.

Slowly draw the skew towards you. Hold the skew steady. At first, this will be somewhat difficult for you. However, with patience and practice, you will do this as naturally as you would push a hand plane.

When I plane with a skew, my right hand holds the far end of the handle and is pressed against my side, between my lowest rib and my hip. (See Illus. 5-12.) This location will vary from person to person and lathe to lathe. Where you press your hand depends on the height of the lathe and your own height. This is a very secure grip, and will hold the skew perfectly rigid.

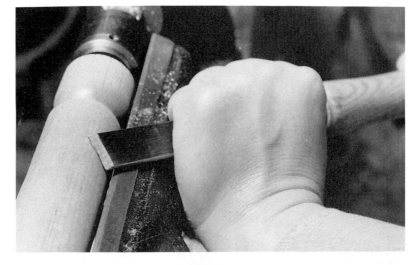

Illus. 5-11. Planing with a skew is one of the more difficult techniques to learn, but the results make it worth the effort. Place the wide side of the skew on the rest with the heel facing the direction of travel (here, right to left). The cutting edge should be skewed at about 65 degrees to the wood's axis. Slowly raise the handle and twist it towards your body, engaging the cutting edge. The heel should not cut, and the toe must not touch the wood.

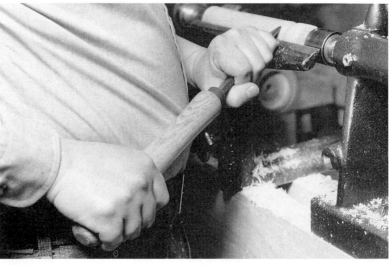

Illus. 5-12. Once you have found the cutting angle, it is critical that you hold the skew steady. One way to brace the tool is to press the handle tightly against your side, just above your hip. Draw the tool towards you.

To move the tool, stand at the far end of the rest with your weight shifted onto your right foot. After the tool has begun to cut, move your torso to the left, gradually shifting your weight back onto both feet (and if the piece is long enough, to your left side).

The cut you make when planing with a skew is very light. The object of planing is to shear a chip off the surface. As you move the skew, you will be able to watch it cut small, gossamer-fine shavings that tend to roll up into tiny, fragile tubes. (See Illus. 5-13.) Complete a pass along the entire length of the blank. Make sure that you keep the skew's pointed nose above the wood. If it makes contact with the wood it will be grabbed and slammed against the rest. You will not be hurt, but you will be startled. Worse, the skew will dig into the wood, creating a blemish that might be too deep for you to remove from the finished turning. This is one reason why beginners are frightened and wary of planing. If you are unsure at all about the procedure, experiment on a practice piece rather than a turning that you hope to complete. With practice, you will be able to plane with ease and complete confidence.

When you have finished planing the cylinder, turn off the lathe and look at it. If you have planed it correctly, it will have a sheen that makes you think you can see right into the wood. The round surface will be as smooth as a freshly planed board.

The grip, stance, and cut just described work well when you are planing from right to left. However, as when planing a board, you have to make sure that you do not plane against the grain of the wood. When turning, always plane "downhill." If the turning has a taper or is a vase, you may not be able to work from right to left because you will be going against the grain ("uphill").

When it is necessary to plane from left to right, you will have to change your grip slightly. The skew's heel always faces the direction of travel, so rotate the blade accordingly. Once again, find the cutting angle by laying the bezel on the wood and lifting the end of the handle. The grip and placement of your left hand will remain the same. Your right hand will still grip the end of the handle, but you will have to move it forward from your side to a point about halfway between your hip and navel. (See Illus. 5-14.) Start planing with your weight on your left foot, and move the tool along the turning by moving your torso and gradually shifting your weight onto your right foot.

If the cylinder you are planing is longer than the tool rest, move the rest to one end and plane as much towards the middle as you can. Next, move the rest so that you can plane the remainder of the turning. Start at the other end and move towards the middle, ending when you have overlapped the planing strokes. (See Illus. 5-15.) When planing a turning, make sure that it is thick enough to withstand

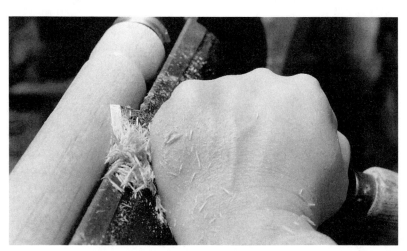

Illus. 5-13. Holding the skew very steady, pull it towards you. Start with your weight on your right foot, and gradually shift it to your left. Make a very light cut. The chips will roll into tiny, fragile tubes. The resulting surface will be as smooth as that left by a sharp hand plane.

Illus. 5-14. To plane from left to right, move the end of the handle to a point about halfway between your hip and navel. Start with your weight on your left foot, gradually shifting it onto your right.

Illus. 5-15. When planing a piece that is longer than the rest, be sure to overlap the planing strokes.

vibration caused by the cutting action of the skew. More often than not, the turning is so thin that it will vibrate when it is being planed. When this happens, the vibrating wood chatters under the pressure of the tool, and the surface is chewed by the cutting edge. The resulting damage is the exact opposite of the effect you are trying to create. The solution is to support the turning from behind with one hand. This will dampen any vibration. Of course, to do this you have to change the way you hold the tool.

So, therefore, if you are planing from left to right, grip the tool in your right hand where the blade and handle join. Grip the blade between your thumb and two forefingers. Wrap your two other fingers around the ferrule and as much of the handle as they will cover.

With your forearm and elbow, press the tool against your side. This locks the tool rigidly in place. Close the fingers of your left hand together, and holding them straight press them against the back of the blank. Remember, if

your hand is cupped over a turning, it can get caught between the wood and the rest. Press your thumb against the upper corner of the skew's blade. This helps control the tool and keeps the thumb out of the way. (See Illus. 5-16.)

Now, because you are gripping the skew against your lower chest, move your body. Draw the skew along the blank, causing it to plane the outline of the turning. When you are moving from left to right, your left hand (which is dampening the vibration) will follow the tool.

If you have to support the turning when planing from right to left, you will not be able to hold the skew with your forearm. Instead, push the end of the handle into your stomach. This is an awkward, but effective position. Your left hand will still support the blank, and your thumb is pressed against the blade's upper corner. However, in this direction your left hand will precede the cutting, rather than follow it. (See Illus. 5-17.)

Both these grips work on elements other

Illus. 5-16. A thin part may vibrate when it is being planed, which will result in a rough surface, rather than a smooth one. When planing from left to right, grip the handle between your body and forearm. Dampen the vibration by pressing your left hand against the back of the part, and pressing your thumb against the blade. Your hand will trail the cut.

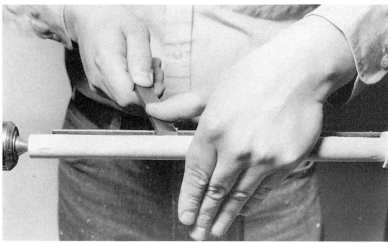

Illus. 5-17. Planing from right to left is somewhat awkward. Brace the handle by pressing it into your belly. Note that your left hand should precede the tool rather than follow it.

than a cylinder and taper. (See Chapter 7.) For example, if you have to plane a vase, start at the apex of the swelling and plane over the shoulder and along the neck. The vase neck is so thin the turning will often vibrate; you will have to dampen this vibration by pressing one hand behind the piece, as described above.

Two final notes of caution: planing is a finishing technique used to smooth the surface of a turning. It should not be used to shape the turning. Also, make the element and then plane it, rather than completing the turning and then returning to finish all the individual sections. This, too, helps to minimize vibration. (See Chapter 8.)

Peeling

Peeling is an advanced technique used to quickly remove wood. It is done very much the same way as planing, only in this operation you purposely engage the skew's heel in the wood. The heel lifts a chip and peels it loose. The chip gathers into a spinning mass of wood fibres that moves ahead of the tool. This mass of chips can become so large that it whips against the back of your hand. (See Illus. 5-18.)

Once again, be careful not to let the toe of the skew engage the wood, for it can grab it. If this happens, you will have the same type of accident that can occur when planing.

Cleaning Up

When you complete an individual element, there are often whiskers of wood remaining between it and the adjacent elements. The skew can also be used to remove these. Snip them off by pushing the skew's heel lightly into the joint. This fine scored line will usually cut the whis-

Illus. 5-18. Peeling is a way to quickly remove wood. It is similar to planing, only you purposely engage the heel. This peels a chip, which remains connected, ahead of the edge. The result is a spinning disc of shavings.

Illus. 5-19. Whiskers of shavings often remain between two elements—in this case, in a shoulder. Remove them by severing the fibres with the heel of a skew.

kers loose. (See Illus. 5-19.) Sometimes the place where these whiskers of wood are located is so tight, you have to use the toe of the skew. If so, turn the tool upside down.

CUTTING WITH A DIAMOND POINT

Some of the operations done by the skew can also be done by the diamond point. A diamond point has an end with two bezels. This end is in essence two one-sided skews combined on the same tool.

Facing Off

You make a face-off cut with a diamond point in a manner similar to that made with a skew. Lay the tool on the edge of its blade, with its flat surface facing towards the shoulder. Place the cutting edge on the blank, just slightly back from the shoulder. Draw the tool's handle rearwards. The lower cutting edge will be lowered into the wood, scoring a fine line. (See Illus. 5-20.) Lift the end of the handle, and push forward slowly at the same time. The edge will shave a wafer-thin disc from the shoulder and leave behind a perfect surface.

Illus. 5-20. To face-off with a diamond point, lay the tool on its edge with the flat surface facing the shoulder. Use the same process used for facing off with a skew. Use a diamond point for delicate jobs, and a skew for heavier ones.

Planing

Because each side of the diamond point is basically a small skew, you can also plane with them. However, these edges are so short they are really only useful for delicate work. Use the same technique used for planing with a skew as described above.

Rolling Cuts

Once again, the cutting edges on a diamond point are small, one-sided skews, and can do the work of skews. The tool can also make rolling cuts. However, only use it for light work, or in a tight place, where its thinner cutting end fits more easily.

V Grooves

The diamond point's nose will cut V grooves. Mark the place where the groove is to be made, and lay the bezel side of the blade on that point. Pull the handle rearwards, sliding the bezels over the wood until the pointed end engages with it. Then, push the tool gently and slowly forward. Make the groove as deep as you wish. This is more of a scraping action than a cutting one, but the detail is so small the difference will not be apparent. This is a quick and effective way to make the rings on bamboo turnings. (See Chapter 7.)

6

BASIC TECHNIQUE

Determining Which Species of Wood to Use

In this chapter I describe the basic steps that occur before the elements can be shaped on a blank. These steps include: determining which species of wood to use, preparing the stock, and rough-rounding the blank. Before you can being to turn a piece, you have to decide what species of wood you are going to use. Almost all woods can be turned, but some turn better than others. Determining the proper species of wood to use is important to cabinetmakers and builders because the piece they select must be structurally sound and carry the load placed on it.

The species of wood a cabinetmaker or builder may ultimately decide to use is determined by several factors. The first factor is the object he is going to make. If he is going to turn balusters for a staircase, they will have different structural requirements than, say, chair legs.

The second factor is the type of wood he wants to use. This is an important factor if he wants to make the project from just one type of wood. Third is the level of detail expected in the finished part. Details can be more crisply incorporated in some woods than in others.

One point should be made about the information given below: I have not turned all the species that might be available where you live. I live in New England, where there is a wide variety of native woods. I have worked with many of these woods, but far from all of them. I can only give you the benefit of my experience, and recommend that you experiment to find the species that works well for you.

Generally, you will turn hardwoods. Hardwoods can be divided into three types: ring porous, diffuse porous, and semi-diffuse porous hardwoods. Ring porous woods include oak, ash and hickory. They are all very hard and strong enough for furniture—even pieces that support the weight of the human body (such as chairs). However, they have very open pores that are clustered in the early wood. (Oak also has a pronounced ray, which results in a fleck on the quarter.) The open pores give these woods a coarse, uneven texture. This texture makes it difficult to turn crisp, sharply

Illus. 6-1. It is difficult to turn sharp, crisp details in a coarsely textured wood such as oak. Such species are better for making round, amorphous shapes, such as the bobbin shown here.

defined details like those needed on a baluster turning. Thus, ring porous woods are good for more amorphous shapes such as bobbins. (See Chapter 7 and Illus. 6-1.)

Ring porous woods all have a strong figure which is very evident under a clear finish. When stained, this figure becomes even more pronounced. However, when painted, the open pores create an undesirable rough texture, unless they are filled first.

Diffuse porous woods include cherry, beech, the maples, and the birches. These woods are also very hard and strong. They also have an even texture which makes it possible to create crisp, sharply defined details. When you have to make highly detailed elements such as rings and discs (see Chapter 7), these woods are a good choice because they are less fragile than ring porous wood. However, because of their even texture, these woods are usually less interesting to look at when turned (except for cherry and curly maple), even when stained. (See Illus. 6-2.) When painted, however, these woods have a smooth finish.

Semi-diffuse porous woods, which include walnut and butternut, also have open pores but they are not clustered in the early wood. They are not as even in texture as diffuse porous woods, and they are not as coarse as ring porous woods. Crisp details can be made in these woods, and they are reasonably strong.

Many exotic (imported) woods also work very well in the lathe. Mahogany is an ideal turning wood (except that the dust makes me sneeze). It is light but strong, and although it has a handsome figure it turns crisply and yields a high degree of detail. I do not have a lot of experience with other exotic woods, and cannot comment on them. If you want to use them, experiment first.

Softwoods (conifers) tend not to turn well. Most common softwoods—pine, spruce, fir, etc.—are too soft to create crisp details. However, they are satisfactory for parts that cannot be seen up close, such as the balusters in a widow's walk. Some hardwoods, such as willow and cottonwood, are also too soft for general use as turned furniture and building parts.

Stock Preparation

As you will learn in Chapter 10, one way to obtain lathe blanks is get them directly from the log using a splitting process called riving. However, most of the turned parts you will use in cabinetmaking and joinery begin as square, sawn blanks. These parts are often called turning squares. Lumber dealers and woodworker supply catalogues sometimes even sell this material under that name.

If your turning will include a square section—for example, the section where a skirt joins it—you have to begin with a turning square (for more information, see below). If you choose to purchase your turning squares (blanks), you will find that these are usually more expensive per board foot than those that you prepare yourself. They can also be more limiting, as you might not be able to obtain the species, the figure, or the dimensions you need for a special project.

Blanks are ordinarily made from a hardwood plank that is 2 inches thick, because many furniture and building parts need to be

Illus. 6-2. Fine-grained woods have an even texture, which makes them the type of wood to use when you want crisp details. However, because of their even texture, they have a less-interesting appearance. The left half of this birch bobbin has been stained, but it is still hard to detect any grain.

turned from 2-inch-square blanks. However, this is not a hard and fast rule. Many furniture spindles are made from blanks 1 inch square, and bedposts and porch columns require 4-inch-square or larger blanks.

If the board you are making into turning squares has any cup to it, begin by jointing one surface. Next, thickness plane the board and joint one edge. Rip the squares so that their width is equal to the thickness of the plank.

You can do all of the above steps in whichever manner you prefer: by machine, by hand, or in a combination of both. However, if the finished turning includes one or more square sections, be sure to clean up all four surfaces of the turning square with a hand plane before beginning to turn. It is sloppy craftsmanship to

leave saw, planer, or jointer marks on your finished turnings, and it is much more difficult to clean up the square sections after the parts have been turned.

To mount the blank in the lathe, you first need to find its centers. Tool catalogues sell devices that do this quickly and automatically. (See Illus. 6-3 and 6-4.) If you intend to do a lot of turning, it would be worthwhile to buy one. However, locating a turning square's center is not a difficult process, and you can do it using tools you already own. Do the following: Lay a straightedge (the blade of a try square will do) on one end of the blank. Align the straightedge with the two opposing corners and trace a line. Next, place the straightedge on the other two corners and draw a second line. This line

Illus. 6-3 and 6-4. These two devices help you find the centers on the ends of either round or square turning blanks (Tools courtesy of Woodcraft Supply)

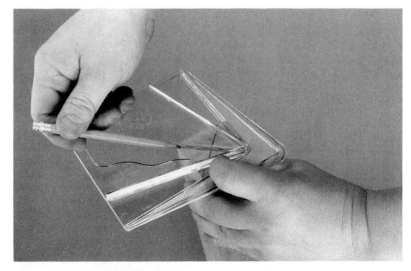

Illus. 6-4.

should intersect with the first one, and form an X. (See Illus. 6-5.) Do the same on the other end. If your blank is truly square (and it will be if made in the manner described above), the intersection of these two lines marks its exact center.

Some turners use a dovetail saw to cut two fine kerfs along the two X lines in one end of the blank. The purpose is to create grooves into which the drive center spurs can be forced, resulting in a surer grip. Other turners knock the spur center loose from the lathe (using a drift), place the center's point on the intersection of the two X's, and, with a mallet, drive the spurs into the end of the blank.

Both these techniques are quite time con-

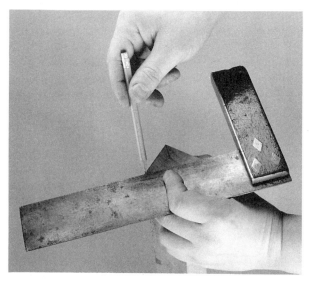

Illus. 6-5. You can also find the centers on a square blank by drawing lines that connect opposing corners. The middle of the X marks the center.

suming, especially if you are making a set of turnings. But, if they make you feel more comfortable using them, it is time well spent. There is, however, one thing you should avoid. Do not leave the drive center in the spindle and use a hammer to drive the blank against it. Over time, this will damage the headstock's bearings.

In the 18 years I made Windsor chairs, I used one method that ensured that the lathe held the blanks tighty enough. I kept the spurs on the center sharp. The pressure of the tail stock made the spurs bite sufficiently, so that the center never loosened or stripped the blank's end grain.

To mount a blank the way I do, first loosen the tool rest and push it towards the headstock to move it out of the way. Line up the drive center's point with the middle of the X. Support the blank with your left hand while you move the tail stock into position. Advance the tail center until its point just enters at the intersection of the second X. (See Illus. 6-6.) The blank is now held loosely in place by the two centers.

Next, lock the tail stock so it will not move on the bed. Then, force the tail center into the blank by advancing the tail stock spindle. The pressure created by the tail center will also cause the spur center to bite securely.

Pull the rest completely out of the way of the blank and turn on the lathe. If the stock is turning either too fast or too slowly (too high or too low RPM), you will have to adjust the position of the drive belt on the pulleys. The

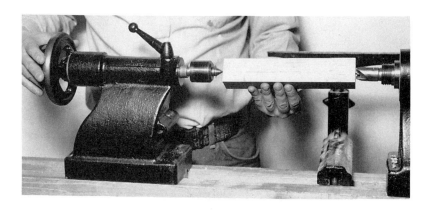

Illus. 6-6. To mount a blank, press the drive center's point into the middle of the X. This will support that end. Hold the other end in your hand and advance the tail center into the middle of that X.

proper speed a blank should turn out is the speed the woodturner feels comfortable with. I prefer to turn at relatively slow speeds, about 800 to 1,000 RPM. I keep my tools very sharp, and I do not need high speeds to make them cut. A beginner should start with a slow speed and increase it slowly to a higher RPM.

There are, of course, other considerations. The thicker a piece of stock, the faster its out-edge is moving and the greater force with which it drives against the tool. So, generally a thick blank should spin at a lower RPM than a thin one.

I once knew a cabinetmaker who would never take time out from a job to sharpen his turning tools. As they dulled, he simply increased the lathe's speed and then cleaned the turnings up by sanding them. Do *not* do this. Learn to sharpen and learn to cut.

As explained in Chapter 1, some lathes are equipped with a dial that allows the operator to select a desired speed. The more common arrangement, however, is two gang pulleys, one in the headstock and the other on the motor. (See Illus. 6-7.)

This is how to use the pulleys to select a desired speed: Place the belt on the larger pulley on the motor, and the belt on the smaller pulley on the spindle. This will give you the highest speed. Conversely, placing the belt on the smaller pulley on the motor, and the belt on the larger pulley on the spindle will create the lathe's slowest possible speed. By varying the positions, you can obtain a variety of RPMs. *Always unplug the lathe before moving the belts.*

You can use the following simple formula to calculate the lathe's approximate speed.

$$\frac{\text{motor pulley's diameter} \times \text{motor RPM}}{\text{headstock pulley's diameter}} = \text{RPM}$$

After adjusting the speed, move the rest close to the blank. Loosen its stem and adjust its height. There is no fixed height for the rest. The goal is to place the cutting edge of the tool so you can achieve the proper cutting angle. (See below and Chapter 5.) For most work (turning 1–2 inches in diameter), the top of the rest should be just below the centerline described by the two centers. You can see this relationship better if you crouch down in front of the lathe until your eyes are level with the top of the rest. (See Illus. 6-9.) When it is parallel to, and slightly below the imaginary centerline that connects the lathe's centers, tighten the handle that locks the rest's stem.

Move the rest into position against the work. It should be parallel to the blank. Before

Illus. 6-7. Adjust the lathe to the speed you prefer by adjusting the belt and pulleys.

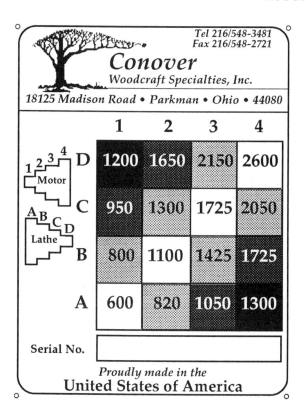

	1	2	3	4
D	1200	1650	2150	2600
C	950	1300	1725	2050
B	800	1100	1425	1725
A	600	820	1050	1300

Illus. 6-8. You can calculate your lathe's speed using the formula given in the text. This chart, which can be found on a lathe manufactured by Conover, identifies the speed at each possible arrangement of the pulleys.

switching on the lathe, spin the blank with your hand to be sure that it will clear the rest. If it does not, its edges will knock against the rest and can be broken off. If this sort of damage were to occur where the blank needs to be left square, you will not be able to use that piece of wood as intended.

Rough-Rounding

The first step in turning is to bring the blank into round. Do not confuse this with the second step, which is turning the blank to a finished diameter. The tool to use in rough-rounding is the roughing gouge. If you do not have a roughing gouge, use a large (¾-inch) spindle gouge.

Illus. 6-9. Before starting to turn, adjust the height of the rest. Crouch down in front of the lathe until your eyes are level with its upper surface. Place the surface so that it is parallel to, and slightly below, the centers.

Lay the gouge on the left-hand end of the rest. Place it on the very bottom of its round blade. This is the position the gouge would naturally find if laid on a flat surface. Grip the end of the handle in your right hand and use an overhand grip (with your left hand) on the blade. The tool is at a right angle to the blank, and its handle is lowered so the bezel will make contact with the blank rather than the cutting edge. (See Illus. 6-10.)

Slowly move the gouge forward towards the rotating stock until the bezel makes contact with the wood. You will hear the corners of the blade knocking against the tool. Slowly draw the handle back while simultaneously raising its end. As you do this, you will lower the cutting edge to the cutting angle. You will note that the cutting edge is at the correct cutting angle when the tool cuts a chip. (For a more thorough explanation of the cutting angle, see Chapter 5.)

When you have found the cutting angle, hold that position and begin to move the gouge slowly and steadily to the right until it reaches the end of the blank. Be sure to also keep the gouge square to the rest. All along the blank you will feel the sharp, rapid knock of the blank's square corners against the tool. Although you should hold the tool firmly, you will notice that contrary to the expectations of most beginning turners, you will not have to fight with the wood.

It is important that when turning you observe what the tool is doing. When *rough rounding*, watch the cutting edge of the tool. In the next chapter, you'll discover that when making other turning cuts, you'll be looking at a different spot.

If you turn off the lathe, you will see that you have cut very short U-shaped chips from the blank's four corners. (See Illus. 6-11.) The chips have been cut clean through from one side to the other, and are short because the blank's corners are so narrow. Repeated passes of the gouge along the spinning blank will further round the corners. As this happens, the cuts (and the chips) will become longer. (See Illus. 6-12.)

Turn the lathe back on and once again find the cutting angle of the tool by lowering the bezel onto the blank and slowly pulling the tool rearward, while simultaneously raising the handle (which lowers the cutting edge so it engages the wood). Continue to find the cutting angle this way until you are familiar enough with the tool that you can automatically determine the cutting angle.

Continue to round the blank's corners using the process described above. While making the first several passes of the tool over the wood, keep your body erect and stationary. Use your arms to move the tool, keeping the gouge at a right angle to the rest with the handle raised to the cutting angle.

Illus. 6-10. To begin rounding the blank, lay the roughing gouge's bezel on the spinning wood. It will knock as each corner rubs against it. Slowly draw the handle rearwards. You will hear and feel the edge cut a chip.

It is important to maintain these angles at this stage of the process. The tool is producing a deeply furrowed surface, but it is also completely severing the chip on both sides of the cut. You do not want to roll the tool yet to make a skewed shearing cut (see below). Though the blank is still nearly square, it is possible for the tool to become caught under the grain and tear a long chip from the square edge. This sort of accident could possibly ruin the blank by tearing wood from below the finished diameter. This would leave a flaw in the finished turning. Also, you do not want large splinters being ripped loose at high speeds. They can possibly hit your knuckles and sting you.

Although you may not notice it right away, after several passes of the roughing gouge the cut has become smoother. This is because the corners have been rounded. Also, you are now taking longer chips that are still shallow and have a U-shape.

It is now time to change motion, so you will no longer hold the gouge in the same manner. Roll the tool on its rounded back about a quarter turn clockwise (so that the left corner of the cutting edge is raised and the blade's round bottom is pointed at about your thigh). This lowers the gouge's outer right edge (where the cutting edge is nearly straight) and puts it in contact with the wood. When the gouge is in

Illus. 6-11. Move the roughing gouge one time along the length of the spinning blank, and shut off the lathe. The corners have been slightly rounded by the gouge, which has made U-shaped cuts.

Illus. 6-12. After several more passes, the blank's corners will become round, and you will notice that the gouge cuts more smoothly.

this position, it will make a shearing skew cut across the wood. (See Illus. 6-13.) You hold a gouge in this position for the same reason you would hold a bench plane slightly askew if you were smoothing a board. As you know from the woodworking you have done on the bench, a cleaner cut can be obtained with a plane if it is held at a slight angle to the wood, rather than being pushed head on. The same principle applies in woodturning.

Holding the cutting edge in this position will give you a smoother cut, but it will also create more resistance against the tool. Rather than fight the tool by locking your wrists and arms, pull your right hand against your body at about the height of your last rib. (This may vary depending on your height and the height of your lathe.) The tool is no longer at a right angle to the work, having been pulled slightly towards you. You can now move it along the spinning blank by shifting your entire body from the ankles and knees, rather than using your arms. With practice, you will naturally develop a smooth swaying motion that is very efficient. At the beginning of each pass, carry your weight on your left leg. As the tool moves along the rest, shift your weight onto your right leg. When you return the tool to the left end of the rest, again transfer your weight onto your left leg. (See Illus. 6-14 and 6-15.)

Pause a moment to observe the chips you are now removing. They are no longer a pronounced U shape. They are thinner and wider than the chips you first cut, and if you hold them up to the light you will notice that they are translucent. They also curl differently. The chips first cut were curled tightly. (See Illus. 6-16.) These curls are more loose. These long shavings are more typical of what you will cut during the remaining operations.

When rough-rounding, you can dramatically increase your efficiency by learning to cut in both directions. You can cut in both directions when rounding the corners and when shearing with the side of the gouge's cutting edge. When rounding the corners, push your arms down the blank, as explained above. Holding the tool in the same position, draw your arms back to you. Do not at any time remove the tool from contact with the wood. You have cut with both motions, both away from and towards you.

When cutting in both directions when shearing, never lift the tool from the wood. As you push the tool away, the blade's round bottom will face towards you at about 8 o'clock. As you reach the end of the blank, roll the tool so that the round bottom is now pointing away from you at about 4 o'clock. Start swaying your body back to the left while simultaneously transferring your weight onto your left foot. Your complete motion will be a rhythmic sway from left to right, and you will be cutting at all times. If

Illus. 6-13. Once the corners are rounded, you can make the roughing gouge cut more efficiently by rolling the tool on its rounded blade about ¼ of a turn. This will create a shearing skew cut.

Illus. 6-14 and 6-15. When rough-rounding, develop a swaying motion. Shift your weight from foot to foot as the gouge travels along the rest, but do not move your feet.

Illus. 6-15.

Illus. 6-16. There is a difference between the first chips a roughing gouge cuts from a turning square and those that are cut as the square becomes more round. The first chips, shown on the left, are very short, and have a U-shaped bottom. Those on the right are longer, having been cut from the rounded corners.

you use this technique, it will take very little time to rough-round a blank.

Throughout the process, the chips will continue to change. When the piece is completely round, the tool is able to cut all the way around the circumference of the blank. The chips will come off as ribbons, breaking only under their own weight rather than breaking because of the flat spots between the corners. (See Illus. 6-17.)

A continuous shaving is one indication that the blank is completely rough-round. You can also lay your hand lightly on the spinning wood and feel it to determine if it is round. Make sure that you hold your fingers flat and barely touch the blank. If you cup your hand, it can be caught, pulled into the rest, and pinched. If you press too hard (or too long), the friction can burn you.

Now that the blank is rough-rounded, you have to round it to its finished diameter (these can also be the same procedures, but are not necessarily so). Set a caliper to the final thickness and, using a shearing cut, move from one end to the other and back again, reducing the turning evenly until the caliper will just fit over the round stock. This is the finished diameter. (See Illus. 6-18.)

There is an alternative way to find the finished diameter: Use a parting tool to make a

Illus. 6-17. When the square is completely round, the chips are cut in even longer strips. Although made with a continuous cut, they have short grain and break up easily.

Illus. 6-18. You can quickly determine the finished diameter by passing a pair of calipers over the spinning blank.

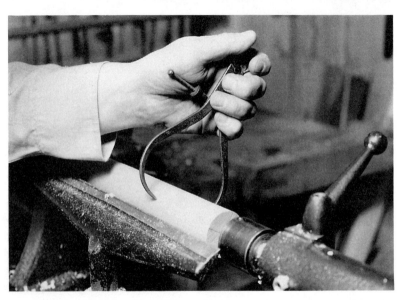

sizing cut. Hold the tool in one hand with the handle locked under your elbow to steady it, and hold the adjusted calipers in your other hand. As you cut the groove with the parting tool, press the calipers against the bottom of the groove. (See Illus. 6-19.) When they slip over the bottom, the groove is as deep as the finished diameter. The groove can now be used as a depth marker.

If you are turning a long cylinder, you may want to make several of these sizing cuts. Round the cylinder to the finished diameter established by these cuts. (See Illus. 6-20.) If you are making many turned parts with one major diameter, mount a sizing tool on your parting tool. (See Chapters 2 and 7.) The

blank being rounded in Illus. 6-10–6-13 was shorter than the tool rest. However, many turnings you need to make will be two to three times longer than the rest. In this case, you cannot round the entire length of the turning at one time.

I use a 12-inch rest, but because the spinning blank can pull a tool off the rest if it gets too close to an end, only about the middle 10 inches of the rest is useful. If a blank is more than 10 inches long but less than approximately 20 inches, I will first rough-round 10 inches on one side of the blank. (See Illus. 6-21A.) Then, I move the rest to the other end of the blank and round that end all the way down to a finished diameter. (See Illus. 6-21B.)

Illus. 6-19. You can determine the finished diameter by making a sizing cut with the parting tool. When you are at the right dimension, the caliper will fit over the bottom of the groove. Use the groove as a depth marker, and rough-round it until it has almost completely disappeared.

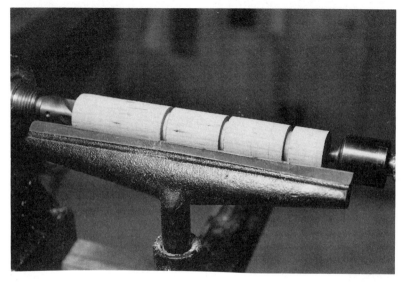

Illus. 6-20. A series of sizing cuts makes it easy to find the finished diameter. Just remove the waste until you have reached the bottoms of the grooves.

Illus. 6-21. If the blank is between 10 and 20 inches long, the most efficient way to bring it to its finished diameter is to do the following: Rough-round 10 inches on one end. Then move the rest and finish-round the other end, as shown at A. Finally, move the rest back to its first position and finish-round that position, as shown at B.

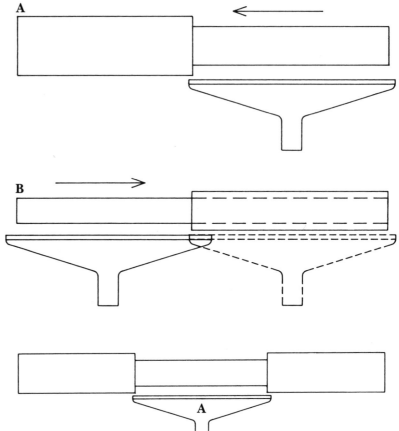

Illus. 6-22. If the blank is more than 20 inches long, the most efficient way to bring it to finished diameter without knocking it out of round is as follows: A) rough-round the middle. B) shift to one end, rough-rounding it. C) shift to the other end, and bring it to finished diameter. D) shift back to the first end and finish-round it. E) return to the middle and finish round-it.

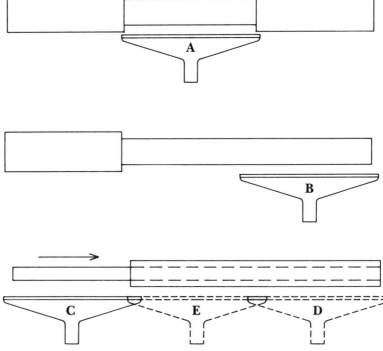

Finally, I return to the first end and round it down to the finished diameter. There is a reason why I use three steps to round the blank to dimension. Rough-rounding creates shock which can knock a blank slightly off its axis, so that it no longer spins perfectly true. If you round the first section to its finished diameter, and then when rough-rounding the second section knock the first slightly out of round, there is no extra thickness left to restore it.

If the blank is longer than approximately 20 inches, the tool rest (remember, I am assuming you are using a 12-inch rest) must be moved at least five times. First rough-round the middle section. (See Illus. 6-22A.) Next, shift to one end (it does not matter which one), and rough-round it. (See Illus. 6-22B.) Then, move to the other end and, in one operation, both rough-round and take it to its finished diameter. (See Illus. 6-22C.) Finally, go back and round the center and then the first end to the finished diameters.

The blank is now its finished diameter. Now you can shape the various elements on it. This process is described in the following chapter.

7

MAKING THE ELEMENTS

Before beginning to turn, you should be able to identify the different elements that you will be learning to make. Many turned elements are similar to the moulding profiles that are used in woodworking. Today's turners do not always use these same terms to describe woodturning elements. This is because the craft of woodturning nearly died out and has only recently been revived. In its new incarnation, the emphasis is on faceplate turning to make art objects. Thus, many of today's turners are unfamiliar with the traditional terms that remain current among builders and cabinetmakers. These terms are listed and described below:

Astragal—A half-round ring that stands above the surrounding surface.

Bamboo—Not really an element, but a series of narrow, shallow coves meant to (depending on the turner's wishes) either merely suggest bamboo's distinctive joints or to simulate the material very closely. In its more sophisticated form, the joints are quite pronounced, the cove being placed between pairs of semi-astragals. Both types of bamboo turnings are sometimes called "false bamboo," or, by the French, *faux bambou*. (See Illus. 7-1.)

Ball—A fully rounded element.

Baluster—Like bamboo, baluster turnings are not strictly an element, but rather a particular group of elements very commonly combined on turnings used in both furniture and architecture. A vase or an urn is the primary element on a baluster turning, and it is usually accompanied by various arrangements of rings and coves.

Illus. 7-1. This false bamboo Fancy chair was made in America around 1815. To further the illusion created by the turnings, the chair was painted the same color yellow as real bamboo. Note that two types of simulated bamboo are used. On the horizontal back rails, there are small bobbins centered by a cove. The stiles have clusters of three evenly spaced astragals.

The vertical elements under a stair's handrail are also called balusters. Since these parts were traditionally an arrangement of vase and other elements, this is probably how the word originated.

Bead—A ring cut into the turning, the apex of its convex shape flush (or near flush) with the surrounding surface. It is a moulding profile similar to an astragal.

Bobbin—A symmetrical swelling.

Cove—A concave ring, which is also a moulding profile.

Cylinder—A length of a constant diameter.

Cyma curves—S-shaped moulding profiles. The cyma recta is a true S shape, concave at the top and convex at the bottom. The cyma reversa is a reverse S, convex at the top and concave at the bottom. These curves are also called ogee curves.

Disc—A wafer-thin element with either a square, rounded, or pointed outer edge.

Fillet (pronounced fill-it)—A small step that sets off a moulding profile or that separates various moulding profiles when used in combinations. Fillets are used for the same purpose in turnings. They separate and define the various elements.

Ring—An element like an astragal, only concave on one side, and convex on the other.

Square—An area of the original turning blank. A square is often strategically placed where a skirt or stretcher is joined to the turned part. In such a case, the mortise is cut into the square. On some parts, such as a table with an H stretcher, the squares are left on the ends of the medial stretcher, and the tenons are cut from them.

Taper—A cone-like element whose diameter decreases in a straight line (or in some cases a nearly straight line) from one end to the other.

Vase—A curved element with a fully rounded bottom and a slender neck. It is really an elongated cyma curve. Lines on a vase flow so that the shoulders (the transition between the body and neck) are also rounded.

Urn—Is similar to a vase. An urn is usually more squat, its body being longer than the neck. Also, the shoulders are angular or pointed rather than flowing.

Following are descriptions of how to make the various elements that were just defined, including which tools to use and what cuts to make. Remember, however, that turning technique varies from turner to turner. As you practice you may develop your own method. As long as they give satisfying results, continue to use them.

Laying Out Square Sections

You now know how to bring a blank to its finished diameter. However, many turned parts require square sections, especially if they are going to be attached with mortises and tenons. If the square is located at one end of the turning, use a soft lead (#2) pencil and a try square to make one line that marks its end. If the square is in the middle of a turning, make two lines to mark both its ends. Many turnings have two or more squares. (See Illus. 7-2.) Lay them out the same way. This work can be done either in or out of the lathe.

When doing any work in the lathe other than turning, make sure that you unplug the motor to prevent it from accidentally starting up and damaging the tools and the work, and injuring you.

After laying out the square(s), adjust the rest and spin the blank by hand to be sure that it will turn clear of the rest. Then turn on the lathe. The lines will flash with every revolution of the blank. This creates a stroboscopic effect so that when you look at the spinning blank you can see these lines clearly, even though they are only flashing. (See Illus. 7-3.)

Next, place a parting tool on the rest in the manner described in Chapter 5. The cut you are about to make must be outside the pencil

Illus. 7-2. Lay out square sections with a try square. Make dark pencil lines, as these are easier to see when the blank is turning.

Illus. 7-3. You can see the lines on a spinning blank even though they are only drawn on one of the four surfaces.

Illus. 7-4. Separate the square with parting cuts.

line; otherwise, the square will be too short by the width of the parting tool blade. Hold the parting tool at a cutting angle and advance it steadily into the spinning blank. The tool will knock as it cuts through the square corners, though it will eventually cut more smoothly as the groove deepens.

In the last chapter, it was suggested that you watch the cutting edge as you turned. In that case, the chips were being cut off in short segments that bounced away from your hand, permitting you a clear view of the action. However, when making elements, you'll find that the shavings are often continuous and pile up on your hand. Also, your hands often get close to the work, which makes it difficult for you to see. For this reason, when shaping elements, it is recommended that you generally only watch the tool's edge until it engages the wood. Then watch the far side of the turning. This area is generally unobstructed, and you can see the blank being shaped, even though the actual cutting is not happening there.

How deeply you cut the groove when laying out a square section depends on the turning. You must not go too deep or the bottom of the groove will remain in the finished piece. It is best to stop just short of the finished depth; this way, the bottom of the groove can be completely removed later.

Test the thickness at the bottom of the groove with a pair of calipers, stopping once or twice to take a measurement. If you are making a number of these plunge cuts, all to the same depth, measure the thickness at the bottom of the groove with a sizing tool attached to the end of the parting tool.

Repeat the plunge cut as many times as is necessary to separate all the squares. Using a roughing gouge as described in Chapter 6, round the areas of the blank outside the squares. The square cutting edge of the roughing gouge will allow you to cut right up to the grooves created by the parting tool. (See Illus. 7-5.) If the finish diameter is smaller than the rough-rounded diameter, turn the blank to its finished diameter. To do this, I will usually switch from the roughing gouge to a spindle gouge.

The spindle gouge will usually create a surface smooth enough to allow you to start shaping the elements. However, if you choose, you can plane the surface with a skew as explained in Chapter 5. If you plane, you will not be able to reach completely into the corner of a square shoulder such as that created by the end of the square section and the parting tool's plunge cut. It is recommended, therefore, that you plane as far as possible and then smooth the remainder with a peeling cut started an inch or

Illus. 7-5. The square corner on a roughing gouge will allow you to cut right into the corner created by a parting cut.

two away from the corner. (The transition from planing to peeling is very natural. Just engage the skew's heel as you approach a corner.) (See Illus. 7-6.)

Before planing, push the heel of the skew into the corner so as to undercut the wood fibres. This way, when you peel into the intersection, the surface cut should be completely clean. However, if there are any stray fibres, snip them off with the skew.

Some squares are left with sharp, right-angled ends, rather than rounded ends. Since the sides of a parting tool plunge cut are rough, the surface should be faced off. Make the facing cut with either a skew or a diamond point. (See Illus. 7-7.)

However, the ends of most squares are rounded because square corners will break when bumped, can catch on clothing, and look unappealing. To round the ends, make a rolled cut with a skew. (See Illus. 7-8.) (This can also be done with a diamond point. I usually use a skew on heavy work, and the thinner diamond point on small squares.) Hold the skew firmly, for you have to cut through the four spinning corners rather than through a complete section. During the first couple of cuts, the skew may be hard to control, and the rolling cut will not be as neat as you want. This should change at approximately the third cut (See Illus. 7-9.)

Illus. 7-6. You cannot plane all the way into a corner. So plane as close as possible and then peel the remaining distance. Snip any stray fibres with the heel of the skew.

Illus. 7-7. Face-off the end of the square with either a skew or a diamond point.

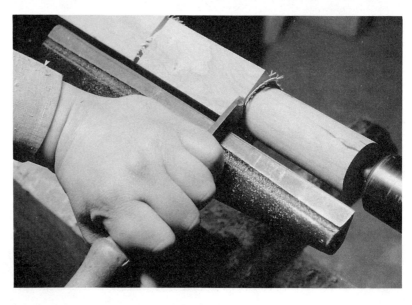

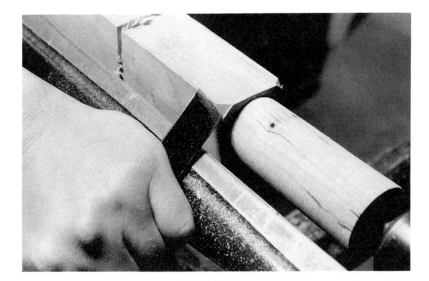

Illus. 7-8. The corners of square sections are often rounded. Round the corners with a skew. The first cuts are difficult because the corners are knocking against the blade.

Illus. 7-9. If you keep the bezel rubbing against the wood, the finished surface will become clean and smooth.

Cylinders

The process of roughing creates a cylinder. However, you usually want a cylinder to have a constant diameter. If the cylinder is short, you can easily check its diameter with a pair of calipers. However, if the cylinder is long, or the same cylinder appears repeatedly on a set of turnings, it is quicker to lay it out with a sizing tool mounted on a parting tool. Set the distance between the parting tool's cutting edge and the inside end of the sizing tool's arm to just slightly more than the finished diameter.

Use a parting tool to make a series of parting cuts along the length of the cylinder. (See Illus. 7-10.) When used with a sizing tool, the parting tool will always cut to exactly the same depth. These grooves are really depth markers. Remove the remaining wood between them with a spindle gouge. Only the barest trace of them should remain, ensuring that the cylinder is a constant diameter all along its length and that it is just slightly thicker than the finished diameter.

Finally, finish the cylinder by planing it with a skew, as explained in Chapter 5. This will remove what remains of the parting cuts and smooth the detail so that sanding will not be necessary.

Illus. 7-10. When you are making a cylinder, a parting tool combined with a sizing tool is very helpful. Make a series of parting cuts that are all of the same depth.

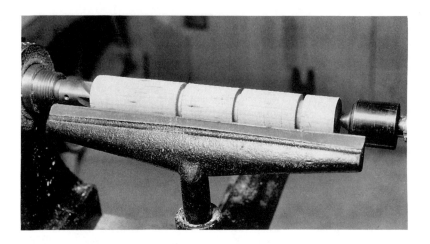

Beads

One of the most common elements used in turning is the bead. A bead is a round detail set off by a groove. The groove can be flat-bottomed (in which case it is called a quirk) or it can have bevelled sides. As a woodworker you know that when a bead is used as a moulding, it is run on a board's corner edge. When turning, a bead is often treated differently, and can have a bevel on just one side or on both sides. (See Illus 7-11.)

When laying out a bead, it is necessary to mark its edges. You can do this with a pencil, or you can make very light scribe marks with the pointed leg on a pair of dividers. You can make quirked beads by laying them out with a parting tool.

Beads are shaped with a skew. First, undercut the sides. Lay the skew on its bottom edge so that the pointed heel formed by the bottom edge of the blade and the sloping cutting edge is aligned with one of the marks. Hold the tool so that it is nearly parallel to the lathe bed, rather than with the handle lowered as is done

when cutting. Line one of the marks up with the skew's heel and push the tool into the rotating wood. Do the same to the other mark. (See Illus. 7-12.)

By following these two steps, you have severed the wood fibres at the two ends of the bead. The profile is now formed between these two cuts. The bead is symmetrical, having two sides which will be formed individually. First form the left side. Place the skew blade so that its wide surface is lying on the rest. Its heel should be aligned with the center of the bead. Use the skew to make a rolling cut. Depending on how narrow the bead is, you may be able to form one side with a single rolling cut. If the job cannot be done with one cut, make two. Start the first cut biased in the direction of the cut. If you keep the lower bezel rubbing on the wood, you will obtain a glassy, smooth surface and the tool will not be grabbed out of control. When making the second rolling cut, move the skew closer to the center of the bead. (See Illus. 7-13.)

If some of the fibres you have severed with the rolling cut remain attached at the bottom of the curve, use the skew's heel to slice them

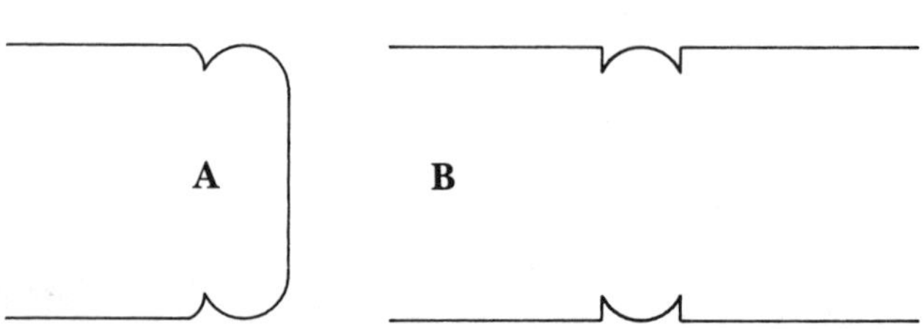

Illus. 7-11. If a bead is placed on the end of a turning, as shown in A, it has just one side, just like a bead moulding. If it is placed anywhere else, as shown in B, a turned bead has to have two sides.

A   B

Illus. 7-12. Lay the bead out by scoring a pair of lines with the heel of a skew.

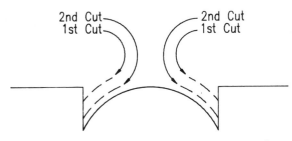

Illus. 7-13. A bead usually requires a minimum of two rolling cuts. Make the first close to the edge, and begin the second nearer to the center.

loose. Do this as you did when scoring the ends of the bead. Reverse the skew and form the other side of the bead by making the same rolling cuts. Only make these cuts in the other direction. (See Illus. 7-14.)

Most of the problems you will encounter when making beads can be resolved with practice. If your cuts produce an inclined plane rather than the arc of a true bead, you are not rolling the tool enough. You may also find that it is difficult to make the second cut a mirror image of the first, and, as a result, the bead is lopsided, rather than symmetrical. Also, you may have a peak where you began the two cuts. Keep practicing, and in a short time you will be able to make perfect beads.

Illus. 7-14. Shape the bead by making rolling cuts in both directions. Keep the bezel rubbing on the wood. This not only gives you better control, you will obtain a glassy, smooth surface.

Coves

The cove is the opposite shape of a bead. In fact, on baluster turnings, the two elements are commonly juxtaposed. This combination results in a common moulding profile, called an astragal and cove (on a turning, a bead usually replaces the astragal). This profile was first developed by the Greeks, who used it in their architecture. It has remained popular in Western woodworking since the Renaissance, and can still be purchased at a lumberyard as stock moulding.

It is recommended that you use a ¼-inch spindle gouge to make coves (unless they are very large). First, lay out the cove's two extreme edges in the same way you did for a bead, using either a pencil or a divider.

Start on the left half of the cove. Lay the gouge on the right edge of its blade so that its hollow throat is facing the cove's center. Lay the point of the "lady finger" cutting edge just inside the layout line. The tool is at 90 degrees to the horizontal, so you will start the cut at the edge of the cove and move towards the middle. (See Illus. 7-15.) At the same time, rotate the blade from its edge onto its round back with your right hand. Your left hand should serve mostly as a pivot.

Bring the cut to the middle of the cove and stop. (See Illus. 7-16.) Next assume the same

Illus. 7-15. Make a small cove with a ¼-inch spindle (lady finger) gouge. Use a larger spindle gouge for larger coves. Start at the side of the cove, with the tool held on the edge of its blade, the hollow surface facing the cove's center.

Illus. 7-16. As the gouge cuts down the wall of the cove, roll it onto the center of its round blade. At the bottom of the cut, the tool should be resting upright. Do not cut any farther, as you risk catching the tool in the end grain in the other side of the cove.

position, but on the opposite side of the cove. The tool should be on its left side, again facing the center. Make the same motion for the first cut, but in the opposite direction.

The two cuts have resulted in a shallow cove. Coves are usually much deeper than can be made in two passes, and you will have to repeat what you have just done several more times. However, begin each cut inside the edges of the cove. If you do not, the cove will grow wider and wider with each cut. You do not want this to occur, as you have already laid out the width of the cove. To avoid this problem, start the tool's cutting edge in slightly from the corner of the cove. (See Illus. 7-17.)

Also, as the cove becomes deeper, you will have to lower the cutting edge of the blade by raising the handle. This ensures that the spindle gouge will remain in contact with the bottom of the cove. Just how much you have to lower the cutting edge is determined by pushing the gouge's bezel against the side of the cove. Throughout each successive pass, keep the bezel rubbing against the cove's hollow sides.

As you make each pair of cuts, be very careful not to extend the cuts beyond the center of the curved bottom. If the edge of the tool makes contact with the cove's opposite wall, it may become caught in the end grain. When this happens, the tool can be pulled out of control. While you will not be hurt, the gouge is usually sent spiralling up the turning, and scars the turning. For this reason, it is advised

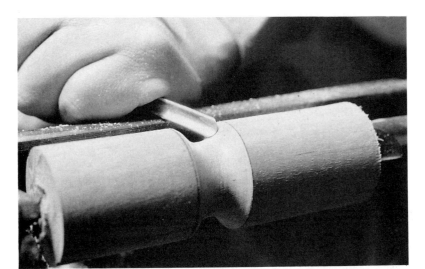

Illus. 7-17. Start each additional cut slightly farther in from the edge of the cove.

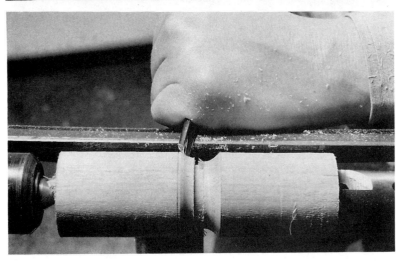

Illus. 7-18. Beginners are often more comfortable learning to make coves by using a parting tool cut. This way, there is no grain at the bottom to catch your tool. When you feel more confident, use the process shown here.

that you learn to make these deep concave cuts in the following way: Make a plunge cut with a parting tool. Practice both your right and left cove cuts on either side of this groove. Since the end grain has been removed, you do not have to worry that the gouge will be caught. (See Illus. 7-18.)

When a cove is placed next to a bead (see above), it is usually separated by a short flat area called a fillet. The cove and bead are usually the same width, and the cove is as deep as the bead is high. Remember, the apex of the bead and the bottom of the cove mark their centers. (See Illus. 7-19.) However, if you follow the procedures just described for making beads and coves, there is no room for the fillet. If you make one anyway, the cove or the bead (or perhaps both) will be asymmetrical.

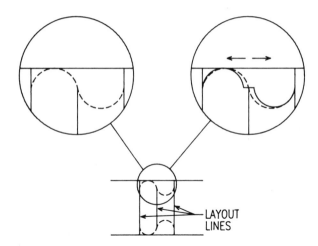

Illus. 7-20. To make room for the fillet, shift both the cove and the bead slightly away from the center.

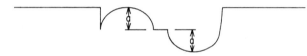

Illus. 7-19. Generally, a cove is as deep as the bead is high. Both are the same width.

To ensure that both the cove and the bead are perfectly shaped, make the bead first. Shift its center slightly away from the area laid out

for the cove. (See Illus. 7-20, in which the bead is to the left of the cove, and the apex is shifted left.) When you cut the cove, shift the center of its bottom slightly away from the bead.

When the cove is finished, create the fillet by making a plunge cut with a ¼-inch skew, as described in Chapter 5. (See Illus. 7-21.) Hold the tool so that its skewed cutting edge is parallel to the tool rest and the axis of the turning. Feed the skew directly into the intersection of the cove and bead. It will cut a perfect fillet.

Illus. 7-21. The fillet between the cove and bead is shaped with a skew.

Vases

If you want to make reproductions of period architecture and furniture, it is essential that you know how to make a vase. Vases are an essential element in baluster turnings. Of course, vases are commonly used in modern turnings, as well.

Vases are made in two steps. In the first step, you form the bottom. In the second step, you make the neck and body. Use a skew to make the bottom. Use rolling cuts. This is almost the exact technique used for cutting beads. The only difference is that beads usually have a shorter radius than the bottom of a vase.

Following are the methods I used to make the vase shown in Illus. 7-22—7-24. As depicted, its bottom points left and its neck faces right. For clarity, I undercut the end of the vase with a skew plunge cut. Usually, you first have to mark the bottom. Score this line by pushing the heel of the skew into the bottom of the vase. Then move slightly to the right, and make a rolling cut with the heel of the skew.

Usually, you cannot cut the entire bottom with a single rolling cut. This is because there is a limit to how thick a chip you can slice off at one time while still controlling the cut. You will have to make several passes. Each time, score the wood fibres at the bottom with the heel of the skew. Then make another rolling cut over the bottom of the vase. Move farther up the vase each time and cut another, longer arc. (See Illus. 7-22.) With each cut, be sure to keep the bezel in contact with the wood. This will not only help control the cut, it will leave a polished, glassy surface.

The design of the vase will determine how many rolling cuts are necessary to form the bottom. Be careful when determining the design. Vases with very round bottoms look squat. Vases with very long bottoms look spindly and fragile.

The rolling cuts should create a polished surface. However, if there is any area on the body between the bottom and where the shoulders will occur that still bears gouge marks, plane that area with a skew.

After shaping the vase's body, make the neck. Obviously, the diameter of the neck will be less than that of the body. To reduce it, use a ¾-inch spindle gouge to make a cut similar to that used to make a cove. The difference here is you do not have to make pairs of cuts, as there is no opposite side. Note that in Illus. 7-23 the finished shape is almost completed. When you are at this stage, your next step is to form the shoulders and complete the vase's attenuated S-shaped outline. Do this with the spindle gouge. The final clean-up is done by planing with the skew, as explained in Chapter 5. (See Illus. 7-24.)

Illus. 7-22. Shape the bottom of a vase by making rolling cuts with a skew. Several passes are usually necessary to complete the shape. Begin each one farther up the vase.

Illus. 7-23. A vase's neck is made in a manner similar to that used to make a cove. However, you cut in just one direction, and you do not have to worry about end grain.

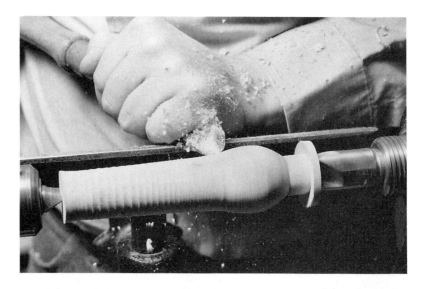

Illus. 7-24. Smooth a vase by planing it with a skew. Note that my left hand is dampening the vibration, as explained in Chapter 5.

Illus. 7-25. The neck on an urn is essentially half a cove, and is cut the same way. Since the urn is usually larger than a cove, you may want to use a larger spindle gouge.

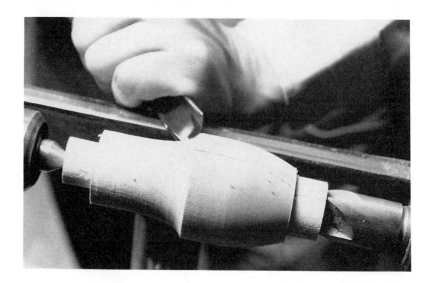

Urns

Tapers

Urns are made very much the same way as vases. The only difference is that the neck of an urn is usually shorter, and its shoulders are not rounded. Shape the neck with cuts with a spindle gouge. Like the neck on a vase, the urn's neck is essentially one half of a cove, and is cut the same way. (See Illus. 7-25.) Because the urn's neck is shorter than a vase's, the gouge should cut it cleanly (as would happen on one side of a cove). Use a skew only to plane any areas of the body that need smoothing.

Tapers are more challenging than vases because their outlines have to be exact. If a vase varies slightly from other vases, this discrepancy is not easy to spot. However, a taper that is not straight is very noticeable.

Making a taper is similar to making the neck of a vase. First, reduce the small end to nearly its finished diameter. (See Illus. 7-26.) The small end on the taper shown in Illus. 7-26 is on the left. To make this taper, move to the right a short distance and, with a gouge, make

Illus. 7-26. Begin a taper by reducing the small end to nearly its finished diameter.

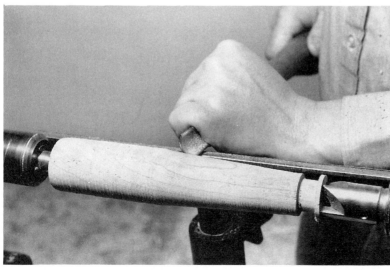

Illus. 7-27. Start each pass farther up the taper. After several passes, the element will begin to take shape.

the same type of cut as you would make when reducing a rough-rounded blank to its finished diameter. Repeat the process, only this time begin even farther up the taper, to the right. Next, make a third pass, starting even farther up the taper. (See Illus. 7-27.)

Each time you make a pass with the gouge, more and more of the taper is formed. The area cut by the first pass has also been cut by the second and third passes. (See Illus. 7-28.)

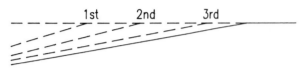

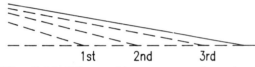

Illus. 7-28. When making a taper, make each pass of the gouge longer than the last. After three passes, the area of the first cut has been cut three times.

As a result, it is the most narrow area. The area covered by the second pass has been only cut twice, and is, therefore, thicker. The area cut by the third pass is the thickest.

Repeat this process as many times as necessary to roughly form the taper. Finish it by planing it with the skew. Move from the thickest area to the narrowest to avoid planing against

the grain. Remember, always plane downhill. If the taper ends in a square corner, peel into the corner with the skew's heel as you would do to the corner created by a square. Finally, snip any stray fibres by undercutting them with the skew's heel.

Astragals

An astragal is very much like a bead. The only difference is that it is not flush with the surrounding wood. Rather, it stands alone. To make an astragal, first lay out its two edges with a pencil or a scribe. With a parting tool and caliper (or, if you are making many identical astragals, a sizing tool), make a groove on either edge. (See Illus. 7-29.) As when laying out squares, make the plunge cuts outside the line.

Next, use a spindle gouge to reduce the turning's diameter on either side of the astragal. This leaves a projecting disc with square corners. Finally, use a skew to make rolling cuts that round the corners, just as if you were making a bead. (See Illus. 7-30.)

Discs

When making the astragal, you first created a short, squat disc. Normally, discs have different proportions than astragals. They have greater

Illus. 7-29. Lay out an astragal's two edges with pencil lines. Then use a parting tool to make a groove on either side of the lines.

Illus. 7-30. Reduce the area on either side of the astragal to the depth of the parting tool grooves. This leaves a short disc, which you round by making rolling cuts with a skew.

height, and are thinner. Otherwise, they are laid out the same way. Use a parting tool to make sizing grooves, and then remove the surrounding wood. Finally, if you want to leave the disc with square corners, clean up its sides by making facing cuts with a diamond point.

You may decide, however, that you want the edges of the disc round. In such a case, round them with a skew, the same way you would round the edges of an astragal. (See Illus. 7-31.) The edge of the disc will have a relatively short radius. Another technique is to use rolling cuts to make edges with a long radius. This gives a disc a peaked edge that is shaped like a

Gothic arch. One of the bedposts shown on page 99 has such a peaked edge.

Because discs are thin, they contain very short lengths of grain. This makes them fragile. A disc can be easily damaged by a blow, which can often break off large segments. (See Illus. 7-32.) Thus, it is wise to take measures to protect a disc when you include one on a turning. One way is to place the disc inside a cove. To do this, first lay out the disc and the sides of the coves with pencil or scribe lines. Cut the edges of the disc with a parting tool. Form the sides of the cove with a spindle gouge, as described above. (See Illus. 7-33.)

Illus. 7-31. A disc is very similar to an astragal, except that it is usually taller. The disc's outer edge can be left square, or can be rounded like an astragal's. It can also be made pointed, in the shape of a Gothic arch.

Illus. 7-32. Discs have very short lengths of grain. This makes them fragile, which is why they are usually protected by an adjacent element.

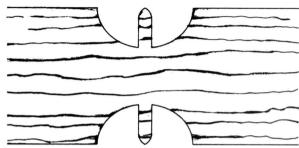

Illus. 7-33. A disc is less likely to be damaged if protected by another element. This one is placed in a cove.

Rings

A ring is also a freestanding element, but it differs from an astragal or a disc in that one side is concave. In baluster turnings, rings are often used at the bottom of a vase. In such a case, begin by cutting the base of the vase. Otherwise, separate the ring with a parting tool, as is done when making an astragal or a disc.

Shape the concave side with a spindle gouge, as you would if cutting a cove. Be sure to leave a little height at the base of the cut to better separate the ring from the surrounding wood. Round the other side with the heel of the skew by using a rolling cut. Be sure to create a crisp cusp at the top of the ring. (See Illus. 7-34.)

Like discs, rings are fragile. They are usually placed lower than surrounding elements. This protects them.

Balls

Like astragals, balls also project above surrounding elements. They are laid out like astragals and discs, except that their width has to be about equal to their thickness. In other words, when making balls in the middle of a turning, lay them out and cut them just like wide astragals.

Balls can be made in one of two ways. They can be formed the way you would form the bottom of a vase: by making rolling cuts with a skew. Several passes will have to be made per side. (See Illus. 7-35.)

Balls can also be made with a gouge. Rough out both sides of the ball, as you would do if making a two-necked vase. Holding the gouge's bezel tightly against the surface of the ball, roll the tool down over the outline of the ball. This action is similar to that used when making a cove, only the outline of the ball is convex instead of concave. (See Illus. 7-36.) Whether I use a skew or a gouge to make a ball depends on the element's diameter. A small ball is easier to do with a skew. I find that using a gouge to make a large ball results in better control.

Balls can be used in the middle of a turning. They can also be used on either end—either as a foot, as shown in Illus. 7-37, or as a finial, as shown in Illus. 7-38. In these cases, you only have to lay out the element's inside edge with the parting tool.

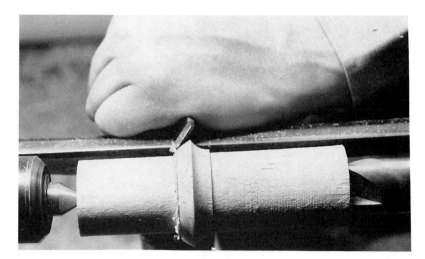

Illus. 7-34. One side of a ring is half of a cove, and it is cut the same way. The other side is half of a bead, and is made with a rolling cut.

Illus. 7-35. Balls can be made in two ways. Smaller ones are made quickly with rolling cuts.

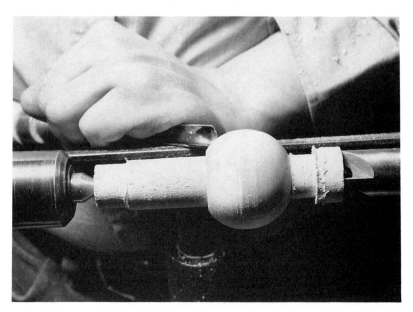

Illus. 7-36. Larger balls are more easily made with a gouge. You will obtain a smooth surface if you make sure that the bezel rubs on the wood.

Illus. 7-37. Balls can be placed on the upper or lower end of a turning. Here one is used as the foot of a Fancy chair leg.

Illus. 7-38. A ball is used as a finial on the stile of this ladder-back chair. The rear surface has been worn flat because it has been repeatedly rubbed against the wall.

Bamboo

In its simplest form, bamboo is merely suggested through shallow, narrow rings made with a ¼-inch spindle gouge. Use the gouge as if you were making small coves. You can also make bamboo with a diamond point. If using a diamond point, make small V grooves instead of rings. Use a scraping rather than cutting action. (See Illus. 7-39.)

A more elaborate form of bamboo is made using two adjoining astragals. Lay out the joint with three evenly spaced lines. Cut the two outside lines and between them with a parting tool, and reduce the surrounding wood to its finished diameter. Rolling cuts made with a skew make the two small astragals. (See Illus. 7-40.)

Another way to make bamboo is to create a series of small bobbins (see below), and mark their centers with small, shallow coves or V grooves. (See Illus. 7-41.)

Bobbins

A bobbin is a symmetrical swelling. This element is very commonly used in turned chair construction; the swelling provides the extra thickness needed to accommodate a joint. In fact, one type of Windsor chair leg is called a "double bobbin" because it has two swellings. The lower swelling provides the extra thickness necessary for the stretcher joint.

Because a bobbin is a symmetrical swelling, it

Illus. 7-39. A simple form of bamboo can be made with a series of V grooves cut with a diamond point. My left hand prevents this part from vibrating.

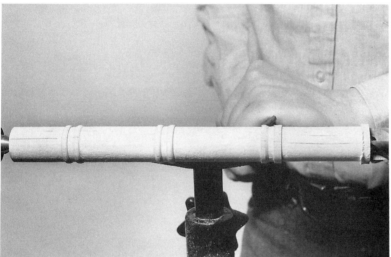

Illus. 7-40. Bamboo can also be suggested with groups of two (sometimes three) astragals.

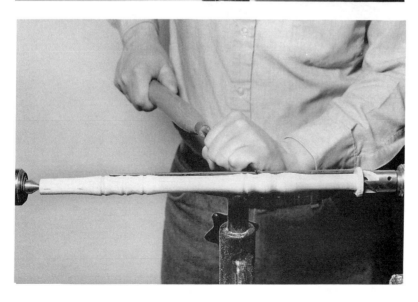

Illus. 7-41. Another form of bamboo results from V grooves made on a series of small bobbins.

is really a mirror image of a vase's neck and shoulder. To make a bobbin, first locate its center with a pencil or a scribe. Next, reduce both of its ends to their finished diameters with a spindle gouge. Using the same tool, shape the shoulders. Smooth the bobbin by planing it with a skew. Work towards both ends from the middle so that you are always planing downhill. (See Illus. 7-42.)

Cyma Curves

S-shaped cyma curves are commonly used as a transitional device on the shoulder between two different diameters. These moulding profiles are more interesting than a simple square shoulder, or even a rounded one.

A long cyma recta (concave at the top) can also be made on the end of a square element. When this happens, the result is an interesting detail called a "lamb's tongue." (See Illus. 7-43.)

Cyma curves are made very much the same ways as urns and vases. However, they are shorter and more compact. To make a cyma recta, first make a layout line. You can add a fillet to the cyma recta if you wish. If you do, it is now considered a stepped cyma reversa. (See Illus. 7-44.) If you include a fillet, cut it first by making a shallow plunge cut with a parting tool. Reduce the concave upper part of the S curve with a spindle gouge, as you would if making a one-sided cove. Use a gouge to "blend" the convex lower curve into the upper curve. (See Illus. 7-45.)

The cyma reversa (convex at the top) can either be set off by a fillet, a quirk, or a bevel. (See Illus. 7–46.) Make this detail first. Both the fillet or the quirk should be cut with a parting tool. Make a bevel with a skew the way you would make one side of a bead. Next, hollow the lower concave curve as you would if making a cove. Finally, "blend" the upper convex curve

Illus. 7-42. When smoothing a bobbin, begin at the center and plane downhill on both sides. Note that I am using my left hand to dampen any vibration.

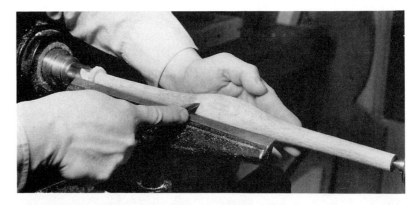

Illus. 7-43. A long cyma recta on the end of a square results in a detail that is sometimes called a "lamb's tongue."

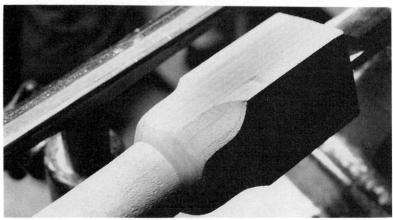

Illus. 7-44. A shows a plain cyma recta. B shows a stepped cyma recta.

Illus. 7-45. Use a gouge to blend the cyma recta's concave upper curve into the convex lower curve.

into the lower with a skew and a spindle gouge. (See Illus. 7-47.)

Fillets

Fillets are the small steps between profiles. They can be either vertical or horizontal. (See Illus. 7-48.) Horizontal fillets are usually most easily made by making a plunge cut with a parting tool or a ¼- or ½-inch skew. (See Chapter 5.) Vertical fillets often start out as the sides of a groove made with a parting tool.

Sanding

If you use your turning tools correctly to cut instead of scraping the wood, most surfaces on the various elements will be cleanly cut. They will have a smoothness that would be ruined rather than improved by sanding. Most people, however, end up doing a lot of sanding, sometimes just because they feel that every piece of wood they work needs to be sanded.

There are two good reasons why you should sand a turning as little as possible. First, a good

Illus. 7-46. A cyma reversa can be set off by either a fillet (A), a quirk (B), or a bevel (C).

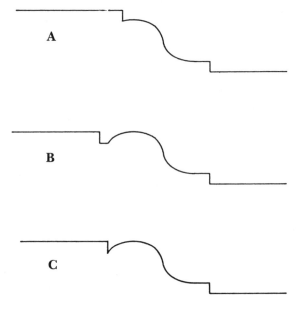

A

B

C

Illus. 7-47. A cyma reversa is also made with a spindle gouge.

HORIZONTAL
FILLET

VERTICAL
FILLETS

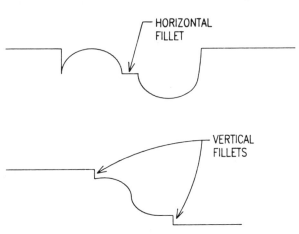

Illus. 7-48. Fillets can either be vertical or horizontal.

turning is crisp. All of its various elements are distinct from each other. Sandpaper will destroy these crisp details.

Secondly, when you touch sandpaper to a turning that is spinning in your lathe, you are sanding across the grain. As a woodworker with some experience sanding, you probably know that sanding should be done in the direction of the wood's grain. Sanding across the grain creates scratches that are very difficult to remove and often reappear under the finish. These scratches become very noticeable when a stain is applied.

When you touch sandpaper to the turning that is spinning in your lathe, you are sanding across the grain. You are creating concentric scratches that can be very difficult to remove, and when you apply a finish you may very well experience the same problems just described.

If you have to sand a completed turning, shut off the lathe and sand along the direction of the grain. Though this may be more time-consuming than sanding a spinning part, you will obtain better results and avoid creating scratches that can mar a turning. In another sense, sanding this way is an advantage. It is such a slow and tedious process, it will make you more determined to develop your cutting skills so that you can avoid sanding altogether.

8

TURNING DESIGN AND PROCEDURE

Whether you are doing woodworking or woodturning, the project has to be designed before it can be begun. Woodturning design is more than just stringing together a series of elements. Here, I will explain some of the factors that should be considered when you are designing turned parts.

Certain elements work better in some arrangements than in others. A good example is the arrangement of panels in both passage (interior) and exterior raised panel doors. (See Illus. 8-1.) Generally, the panels run vertically, rather than horizontally. Small square panels are either placed under the top rail (and are colloquially called Christian doors, since the stiles and rails form a cross), or in the middle at about the height of the lock. A door very seldom has small panels at the bottom because this is a visually unappealing arrangement. This same principle applies to woodturning in that some turned elements make better design sense when used together than with others.

There is yet another factor that should be considered when you are designing turnings. Just as the form of a table or door is largely determined by its function, so too is a turning's design often influenced by its purpose. A table leg will look different from a staircase newel, and a chair stretcher will not look like a pedestal on a tripod table.

The best way to develop a sense of what elements work well together, and in what proportions, is to see what other turners have done in the past. Look through some books of period furniture and architecture. (See the Bibliogra-

Illus. 8-1. Just as the panels in a raised panel door have a usual arrangement, so do the elements on a turning.

phy on page 187.) Sadly, the woodturning and woodworking practiced and taught today places too little value on studying what was done in the past. This is unfortunate. Through trial and error, old-time turners worked out successful designs that have withstood the test of time. If you choose to study their work, you will not only be the recipient of these successful designs, but you will also be able to avoid making any mistakes they may have made years ago. After all, what did not look good in the past will not look any better today.

By looking at work from different furniture and architectural periods, you will note that turnings changed over time. During each period, certain combinations of elements were accentuated. The turned legs on a William and Mary period table (late 1600's) are very different from Sheraton period (early 1800's) legs. (See Illus. 8-2 and 8-3.) The balusters used on

a Georgian period (1750-1800) staircase are very different from those on a Victorian staircase. (See Illus. 8-4 and 8-5.) A knowledge of these differences is very important for woodworkers who make reproduction furniture or build period houses.

Even if you are doing your own designing instead of reproducing, there is much you can learn by studying past woodturnings. For example, the Sheraton style, with its emphasis on delicacy, is an ideal style to adopt if you want to convey a light and airy look to your turnings. Illus. 8-3 shows a leg from a Sheraton-style card table made in the Portsmouth, New Hampshire area around 1805. The turner placed the greatest mass at the top of the turning, so the turning grows thinner as it approaches the floor. The leg's major element is a long, attenuated vase with its body upside down.

Illus. 8-2. Each furniture and architectural period had its own particular style of turnings. Since there are only a limited number of elements, it was the scaling and combinations of elements that changed from period to period. Although vases are used on many of the turnings shown in this chapter, note how they differ. This turning is a William and Mary period table leg (c. 1720) and is symmetrical in that the bottom and upper halves are the same. This arrangement is not common in most other periods.

Illus. 8-3. Legs from a Sheraton-period card table (c. 1805).

Illus. 8-4. Georgian-period stair balusters in the Wentworth-Gardner House, Portsmouth, New Hampshire (c. 1760).

Illus. 8-5. Stair balusters in a Victorian house (c. 1890).

On the other hand, if you want to convey stability, study Chippendale-style furniture, which is much more robust than Sheraton-style furniture. Illus. 8-6 shows the pedestal of a Chippendale tea table made in Boston, Massachusetts around 1790. The major element is once again a vase. However, this vase is placed upright so that the viewer sees the vase's 3½-inch-diameter body below the tabletop. In other words, when designing the pedestal the turner placed the weight at the bottom. Also, the vase is short and squat, rather than attenuated, as is the vase on the Sheraton table leg.

When trying to make a turning, whether it is robust or delicate, remember that certain elements themselves define certain looks. Gener-ally, convex elements will appear more robust, while concave ones look delicate. You can alter a turning's effect by using more concave than convex elements, and vice versa. Illus. 8-7 shows three low bedposts. Overall, the middle post appears more delicate than the other two. This is largely done by using concave elements.

A well-designed turning will terminate in a logical manner. A leg should have a foot, while a freestanding upright part, such as a bedpost, should have a finial. Finials and feet too, affect a turning's design. For example, note the different feelings conveyed by the bedposts shown in Illus. 8-8. These beds were made around 1820. One is a low-post bed. The other is a high post or canopy bed. The low-post bed

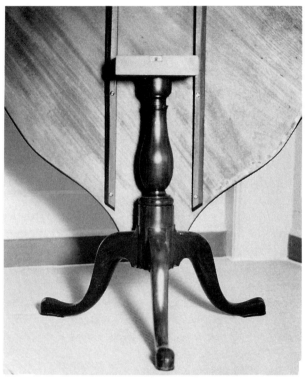

Illus. 8-6. The vase on this Chippendale-period (c. 1790) tip-top tea table is robust and conveys stability.

Illus. 8-7. Concave elements appear more delicate than those that are convex. Compare these three bedposts of the type coloquially called "cannon ball" or sometimes "bell and ball." The one in the middle appears much lighter and more delicate than the others.

Illus. 8-8. Note how the finials on these bedposts affect their appearances. Although the low bedpost is more delicate overall, the ball finial makes it look more substantial than the high post. The iron spindle on the top of the high post holds the canopy.

ends in a ball finial. This type of bed is colloquially called a "cannon ball" or "bell and ball" bed. Even though the post is itself very delicate, the ball-shaped termination gives it a feeling of greater substance. On the other hand, the high-post bed ends in a vase, which creates a more delicate impression, even though the overall turning is heavier.

As a general rule, turned elements that are placed horizontally are symmetrical. (See Illus. 8-9.) In other words, they divide evenly in the middle so that their two ends are mirror images of each other. (See Chapter 13 for a discussion of barley twists). Horizontal turnings are most commonly used for stretchers, the parts that connect and strengthen furniture legs. Stretchers are normally used on tables, chairs and desk frames. These types of furniture are themselves symmetrical, and an asymmetrical stretcher would disrupt their designs.

Symmetrical turnings can also be used as vertical elements. For example, William and Mary table legs commonly featured symmetrical turnings. (See Illus. 8-2.)

Be aware of spacing when designing a turned part. Including too many elements onto a turning can make it look busy. If the part is made up of the same type of element, give each element sufficient space, or the effect can be overwhelming. (See Illus. 8-10 and 8-11.)

Another factor to consider is proportion. The turning should be in proportion with the work of which it is part. Also, the elements on a turning should all be in scale with one another. Finally, each individual element should be of the proper proportion.

Some Windsor chairmakers, influenced by the well-known furniture critic Wallace Nutting, disregard all three of these rules, just as he did. Nutting, whose factory produced reproduction Windsors (as well as other furniture) back in the 1920's, was fascinated by exaggerated turnings. (See Illus. 8-12.) In fact, his turned parts were so bold that they overwhelmed his chairs, violating the first rule of proportion. Ignoring the second rule, he also placed thick vases above very deep coves. The cove's deepness made it appear very slender, and the vase even wider.

Finally, violating the third rule, he made the necks on these wide-bodied vases very slender. As a result, Nutting's chairs are almost caricatures of the original Windsor chairs, looking like they are all leg.

Generally, each of the elements in a turning should be distinct, with crisp delineations. This makes the turning look like it was assembled

Illus. 8-9. Horizontal turnings are usually symmetrical, as is this front stretcher on a banister-back chair (c. 1720). I can only think of one exception to this rule—the side stretchers on some high-style Queen Anne chairs.

Illus. 8-10. Be aware of spacing. Too many elements crowded together or repeated too often make the piece look busy. Shown here is the back of a common Spanish chair (c. 1890).

Illus. 8-11. The elements on this Cromwellian chair (c. 1670) are also crowded.

Illus. 8-12. Wallace Nutting Windsor chairs have bold, crisp turnings. However, Nutting was not as attentive to scale as were early Windsor chairmakers. (Photo courtesy of Michael Ivankovich Antiques)

from separate parts. Fillets and rings are very effective devices for distinguishing one element from another. The elements used on the bedposts and baluster Windsor chair leg shown in Illus. 8-8 and 8-13 are distinct. Fillets were used very effectively in these cases.

A very different effect—a softer and more amorphous one—is created when the elements on a turning are made to flow one into the other without distinction or interruption. Compare the double bobbin Windsor leg, the foot stool, and the "sausage and ring" ladder-back chair shown in Illus. 8-14–8-16 with the two bedposts and the baluster Windsor leg shown in Illus. 8-8 and 8-13.

Another factor to consider when designing a turning is that wood has its limitations. If you do not work within these limitations, you may regret the results. For example, as mentioned, a Sheraton period turning is delicate—that is, light and airy. But it is not fragile. However, some elements that help create a light and airy feeling are fragile. Some examples are discs and rings. They have very short lengths of edge grain, so virtually any blow can break them. If you try to incorporate these delicate elements improperly, they may not stand up well over time.

Yet, in the proper application, these fragile elements also help give a turning a light and airy appearance. So, when using them take the proper steps to protect them. As explained in

Illus. 8-13. Turnings should be crisp and distinct, such as the turnings on this Windsor chair leg. Much of the crispness is the result of fillets.

Illus. 8-14. When there are no fillets, the elements on a turning flow into each other and create a softer and more amorphous effect. Compare this double-bobbin Windsor leg with the baluster leg shown in Illus. 8-13.

Illus. 8-15 and 8-16. The same effect is created by the turnings on the ladder-back chair, on the left, coloquially called a "sausage and ring" chair, and by the legs on this foot stool.

Chapter 7, it is best to place them under an element (or between elements) that projects higher than they do. An example of this is the ring under the vase on a Windsor chair leg. Another solution is to place them inside a concave element. The turner who made the low bedpost shown in Illus. 8-8 placed a disc in a deep cove.

There are other limitations to wood as applies to woodturning design. Some turned parts, like chair legs, support heavy loads. If they are too thin, they can break. Wood also crushes, so the foot of a chair leg should not be so small that its bottom end mushrooms under the weight it must carry.

One obvious consideration that should still be noted is that the woodturning should be designed so that there is no risk that anyone or anything that interacts with it will be hurt or damaged. Consider a very thin, pointed foot on a chair leg. The leg most likely will not be capable of supporting a lot of weight, and might be crushed. The narrow foot also can damage the floor. Finally, the weight of a person sitting in the chair will drive the small pointed ends of the legs into linoleum, carpet, or wood.

Also consider the safety and comfort of people when you are designing a turned part. For example, avoid sharp corners and edges where people will come into contact with your turnings. If you are making stair balusters with square sections, round their ends so that they cannot snag on clothing. Do not include sharp corners on table legs, as they could tear pants or nylon stockings.

When designing turnings, always keep in mind the old adage, "form follows function." In other words, the job the turning performs determines to a great extent what it looks like. Look again at the pedestal of the Chippendale tea table shown in Illus. 8-6. Its tripod base is made possible by a heavy cylinder called a "boss," into which the legs are joined with sliding dovetail tenons. The boss ensures that the joints are strong enough to endure daily use.

Likewise, each of the turned sections of the dumbwaiter shown in Illus. 8-17 also has a boss. Rather than serving to accommodate leg joints, each of these bosses is bored and threaded so that it can screw onto the threaded tenon on the top end of the lower section. These bosses, too, are essential.

The same principle applies to the squares at the top and near the bottom of the William and Mary table shown in Illus. 8-2. The squares are mortised to accommodate the skirt and stretcher tenons. Note, too, how the corner on the Windsor chair stile fits into a notch at the

Illus. 8-17. The bosses on the bottoms of the two upper turnings of this Chippendale dumbwaiter have to be robust in that they contain a wooden nut into which the threaded top of the lower section is screwed. The legs are dovetailed into the lowest boss, as they are on the Chippendale table shown in Illus. 8-6.

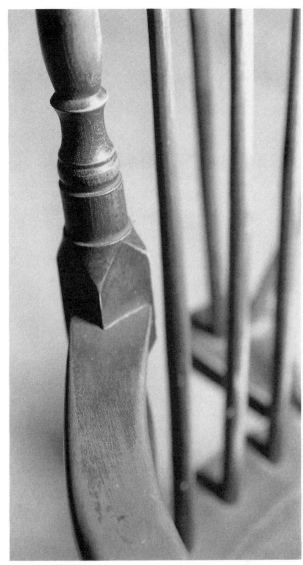

Illus. 8-18. The square on this fan-back Windsor chair stile is strategically placed to form a joint with the arm.

end of the arm. (See Illus. 8-18.) Also note that the lower bobbin on the Windsor chair leg (Illus. 8-14) is larger than the upper bobbin. There is a reason for this: It has a hole drilled into it to receive the stretcher tenon.

The turned newel post shown in Illus. 8-19 has to be massive because it provides the anchor for the stair banister. On the other hand, the balusters serve only to fill the space between the treads and hand rail. Because they are mostly decorative, they are light and delicate.

Illus. 8-19. Even though this newel post at the Wentworth-Gardner House is both pierced and carved to look more delicate, it is much more robust than the balusters. It has to be, as it is the anchor for the banister.

Executing a Design

Once you have designed your turning, you have to execute it.

Your natural inclination will be to round the blank and to then start shaping elements at one end of the turning, progressing steadily to the other. This is, in fact, usually the wrong approach to take. It will weaken the blank so that it vibrates. Vibration is caused when the blank actually bows (ever so slightly) under the pressure of the tool. It bows with each revolution, creating a vibration. The result is a roughly cut surface disfigured by chatter marks. (See Illus. 8-20.)

The wood you are turning is only as strong in its resistance to bowing as is its smallest diameter. In other words, if you are turning a two-inch-diameter blank that is 18 inches long, it will be quite strong and stiff. However, if you were to cut into the blank a deep cove that is only ¾ inch thick at its bottom, the blank will no longer be as stiff and resistant to vibration. If the cove is the first element you cut into the blank, you will encounter a lot of vibration when you make the rest of the elements.

Heavy vibration can knock the turning out of round. When this happens, basically the only sound option you have is to run the incomplete part through the wood stove.

Thus, it is advisable to begin executing a turning by shaping the elements in the middle of the turning and working simultaneously towards the two ends. This means that you will have to move back and forth along the turning, but it does minimize the amount of vibration you will experience and will make turning more pleasurable.

If the turning has several different major finish diameters, it is best to create these after rough-rounding rather than when you start to shape the elements. A good example of this is a baluster Windsor chair leg, of which I have turned literally thousands. The leg has two vases. The one in the middle of the turning is substantially larger than the one at the top.

Illus. 8-20. If you begin a turning at one end and work towards the other, you weaken the blank so that it vibrates under the pressure of the turning tools. The result is chatter, which disfigures the work.

The leg's maximum diameter along its mid-point occurs on the body of the large vase, while the maximum diameter at the top is established by the body of the small one.

When starting the leg, it is best to rough-round the blank and then round it to its larger and smaller finish diameters, instead of to just the larger diameter. You can determine these two diameters by measuring the two vases on the turning with calipers. After creating these two diameters, you are ready to cut the various elements that comprise the leg.

If, instead, you were to round the blank to just its larger diameter and then begin to shape the elements, you would eventually have to cut away the excess wood at the top. Whenever there is a lot of wood to be removed, it is most efficient to do this in the fastest way possible. In turning, this means either using a roughing gouge or your largest spindle gouge, as these tools cut the thickest chips.

However, the heavier the cut, the more pressure the tool creates. The more pressure created, the greater the bowing and the resulting vibration. Thus, beginning the turning and then using a heavy tool to get rid of the waste wood at the top risks causing vibration that can knock the partially completed part out of round and wasting the work and money you invested in the project. The only way to avoid this risk would be to remove the excess wood with a small lady finger gouge that does not take a heavy cut and does not cause excessive vibration. However, this greatly increases the amount of time required to make the turning. Thus, rounding the blank to just the larger diameter and then shaping the elements has created a no-win situation for you.

Obviously, there is no set procedure to follow all the time. Each process is different, and the instructions given for making parts are only general ones. Think about the process you will follow before beginning. Practice different procedures. Through trial and error, you may find even more effective procedures.

Illus. 8-21–8-26 show the step-by-step procedures I used to make a baluster Windsor chair leg. I have made this particular type of leg for over 19 years and these procedures have evolved over that time span. It is hoped that they will prove to be a general model for you when planning your own woodturning procedures.

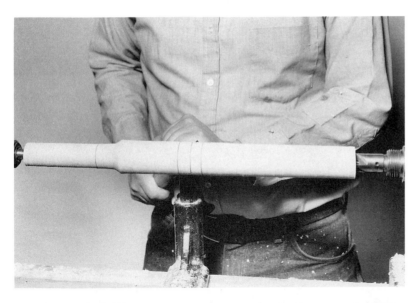

Illus. 8-21—8-26. The procedures I use for turning a Windsor chair leg. Here I am rounding the blank to its two finished diameters, and locating four locations along its length. The rest is placed in the middle of the blank.

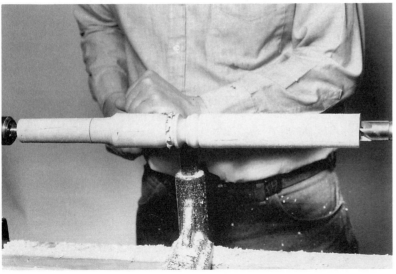

Illus. 8-22. The cove and bead and the ring in the center are shaped, as is the bottom of the larger vase.

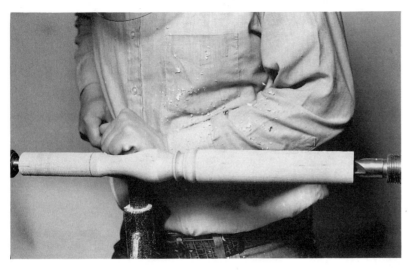

Illus. 8-23. The neck of the vase is cut.

Illus. 8-24. The ring at the top of the large vase is made.

Illus. 8-25. The bottom of the small vase is cut. The rest is moved to the left, and the taper is formed.

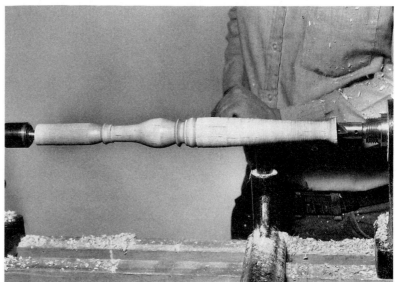

Illus. 8-26. The rest is moved to the right and the neck of the small vase and the tenon are made.

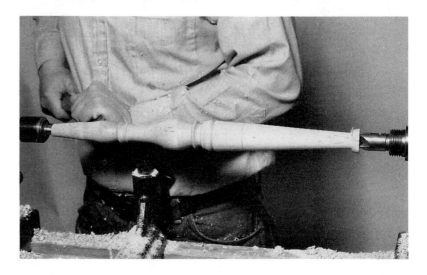

9

DUPLICATING

Turned parts made in a factory on a back-knife lathe are all identical. Since most woodturning is done in factories, most of the turnings we see in our everyday lives have been mass-produced. Because machine-made turned parts are omnipresent in our society, they have become a sort of benchmark. Unwittingly, many turners allow these mass-produced, factory-made turnings to establish the standard on which they base their own work.

You can avoid this mistake if you will take a minute to compare a hand-made turning to a similar factory-made turning. (See Illus. 9-1.) The differences are obvious. The elements on the hand-turning are crisp and clean because the turning tools have smoothed their surfaces. The elements are all fully developed and distinct from each other, and they move dramatically and gracefully from thick to thin.

On the factory turning, there is far less contrast between the thick and thin elements. Also, the details are rounded and blunt. The turning is soft, amorphous, and is larger in diameter than it should be. It is also covered with a matte of fine scratches. This is because the back knife cannot cut the wood cleanly. Instead, it grinds the wood away, and the turning has to be heavily sanded to make it smooth.

In short, the factory-made turning is inferior to the hand-made one. The only positive thing that can be said about it is that it is identical to all those made before it and after it. The poor level of workmanship evident in factory-made turnings should not set the standards for you.

Obviously, when turning sets of furniture or building parts for use in your woodworking, you should try to make them all identical. However, when turning by hand, exact duplication is more an ideal than a reality. Fortunately, your success is judged by the human eye, which has a limited ability to detect the level of variation that normally occurs in hand turnings. In fact, the eye seems to expect duplication, and for this reason it will not detect some astounding differences. Your inconsistencies will have to be glaring before they become noticeable. The chair shown in Illus. 9-2 is a good example. Having made Windsor chairs for so many years, I am aware of the differences in the diameters of the chair's two front legs, but of all the people who have seen it and admired it, no one else has spotted the problem. Their eyes see two legs of the same diameter.

This is one principle at work here that may partially explain why the discrepancy between the diameters remains undetected. The farther apart turnings are one from another, the harder it is for the eye to compare them.

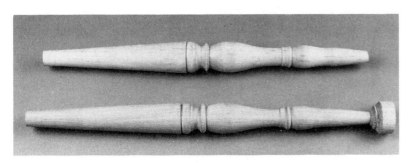

Illus. 9-1. Compare the hand-turned baluster Windsor leg on the bottom to the mass-produced one made in a factory on a back-knife lathe. The elements on the hand-turned leg are crisp and sharp. The elements on the factory-made leg are soft and rounded.

Illus. 9-2. The large vase on the left leg of this hand-made Windsor chair is 5/16 inch thicker than the vase on the right leg. In spite of such a large variation, no one ever notices it unless it is pointed out to him.

Therefore, you have more leeway when making a set of dining table legs than when making a chair. Similarly, a row of balusters for a railing (parts that are closely spaced in a row) have to be more similar.

However, even this rule is not hard and fast. The distance from which the parts are meant to be viewed also plays a signficant role. A roof balustrade (often called a "widow's walk") is placed two or three stories higher than the viewer and, therefore, its balusters do not have to be as perfect as the balusters on a stair landing which are observed from only a couple of feet away.

A similar situation exists when the identical element occurs more than once on a single turning. It is difficult for the eye to compare the same element when it is repeated at the top and at the bottom of a part. They are too far from each other. On the other hand, a bobbin (which seems like such a simple element to make) presents difficulties. It is symmetrical, and any discrepancies between one side and the other are more apparent than if the two ends were separated.

When making parts in the lathe, there are, of course, situations where you have no margin for error, as, for example, when making a set of legs for a table that has both a skirt and stretcher. The squares all have to occur at the same height or the stretcher will be distorted (if it fits at all). However, should the neck of a vase on one leg have a slightly different curve than the vase neck on another leg, the discrepancy will probably never be noticed by anyone other than the most determined critic; someone who is that intent on finding a reason to criticize your work will notice something else first.

More concern than necessary is placed on duplication, and most duplication methods are much more complicated than they need to be. In years past, when hand turners provided the various building and furniture trades with huge quantities of turned parts, most of the duplication was seemingly done by eye or with help from very simple devices. Unfortunately, these devices have not survived so that they can be studied and recorded.

My own experience points out how simple duplication can be. For years, I turned baluster Windsor chair legs mostly by eye. As I show in Chapter 8, I only needed to find two diameters and two locations. After that, I did all the duplication with the help of two gauges—my eyes.

It takes awhile to learn how to duplicate by sight though not anywhere near as long as you might think. In the meanwhile, you may find one or more of the techniques described below helpful. Do not hesitate to adapt other methods to suit your preferences.

Before I describe duplicating techniques, there is one important point that should be made: If you receive any tool catalogues, or have attended any of the woodworking trade shows held in major cities around the country, you have probably seen a lathe duplicator for sale. Many manufacturers make these devices. They are mounted onto a lathe to help make duplicate turnings.

Most lathe duplicators trace a pattern from a master turning. They work on the same principle as a pantograph. A moving stylus follows the outline of the original, while controlling a cutter that travels along the spinning blank.

These duplicators are popular, but are not really very useful. They do not give you either the detail quality or surface that results from hand turning. In fact, the surfaces cut by a lathe duplicator are usually very rough and coarse.

Those who sell lathe duplicators argue that the duplicator should do the rough work for you so that you can concentrate on the finish work. This sounds reasonable, but the real skill in turning is in the finish *and* rough work. And long before you are able to do finish work, you will have learned to do the rough work much more quickly than can a duplicator. This is why I suspect many of the duplicators that are sold are not being used. You are better off practicing and learning to turn with confidence, accuracy, and speed.

One of the most commonly recommended devices for duplicating (probably more commonly described than actually used) is the reverse template. In concept, this device is similar to that of the movable-finger, profile gauge—a tool you can buy in any hardware store. When a profile gauge is pushed against an outline of a moulding or a turning, it makes a reverse copy of the profile. (See Illus. 9-3.) A reverse template is also a reverse profile of the turning you want to make. The only difference is it is permanent, while you can eliminate the impression the gauge makes by realigning its fingers.

The template is usually made by copying the outline of the turned part from a measured drawing onto a thin, hard, homogenous material like plastic. It is then cut out with a utility knife. When the template's contoured edge is held up to the spinning part, you can compare the profile you are making with the original. (See Illus. 9-4.)

Such templates have several disadvantages. First, they require a lot of time and work to make, and that amount of effort can only be justified if you are going to produce a large number of that particular turning. Second, the template's profile cannot perfectly duplicate the crisp details that you can produce in a hand turning. Therefore, if you are going to use the template to duplicate parts, you will diminish the quality of your turning. If you decide only to rely on the template as a guide, there is really no reason to use it at all.

Third, if you tried to use a reverse template on a turning with square sections it would be knocked out of your hands, unless you turn off the lathe every time you check the accuracy of the turning.

For these reasons, many turners prefer to make a more simple form of template when

Illus. 9-3. When pushed against a turning, a profile gauge makes a reverse copy of the profile. However, a profile gauge is not accurate enough for delicate or highly detailed work.

Illus. 9-4. A reverse-profile template is similar to a profile gauge, only it makes a permanent copy.

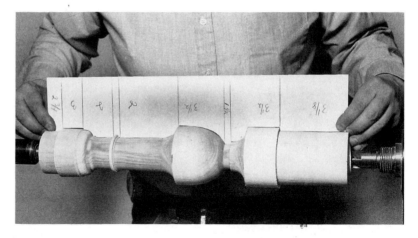

duplicating. It is no more than a narrow board with a straight edge. Along the edge are marked the limits (the beginnings and endings) of the turning's various details.

To use this template, hold it up to the spinning, rounded blank and transfer the limits from the template to the blank with a pencil. To make this an easier and more exact process, some turners cut V notches that are centered on each line. (See Illus. 9-5.) An hexagonal pencil centers itself in such a notch, making it easier to transfer the information accurately.

When making such a template for a very simple turning (one that does not include a lot of different diameters), you can insert the sharp ends of nails at these critical points. When you push the template against the spinning blank, these points will mark or score all these lines at once.

Using a fine-point ink pen, you can also write on the template any other pertinent information you need for duplicating that turned part. For example, you might make a record of the turning's various diameters. This way, you always have these measurements handy when you are setting your calipers.

This type of template is the turner's equivalent of a storyboard (sometimes called a story stick) that carpenters occasionally use when laying out interior trim, or spacing clapboards. The template really does not help you to make duplicate shapes. Rather, it brings together for quick reference all the information you need for laying out a turning that you make frequently.

A similar technique can be used when you are making parts that include square sections, such as occurs on a table leg where the skirt

Illus. 9-5. A story board template locates critical points along the turning's length. You can note critical diameters on the template, but you still have to set the calipers from a ruler.

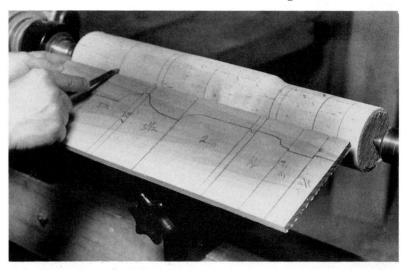

and stretchers are joined. Lay all your turning squares together and line up the ends. It may help to hold them in a clamp so that they cannot shift. Locate the limits of the square sections on one blank, and, using a large try square, continue the layout lines across the remaining blanks. (See Illus. 9-6.) Once again, this technique does not help you to make more exact duplicates. Rather, it helps speed up the process.

I use another technique for duplicating, one that combines many of the concepts just described, but is more sophisticated. Whenever I have to make a turned part for the first time (whether reproducing or designing my own), I make a turning that I designate as the model.

I use the model turning in the same manner as the simple storyboard template described above. I set the model against the revolving blank and, by placing a pointed scribe (I use one leg of a divider, but you can also use a pencil) at critical points, transfer the locations of the various elements. (See Illus. 9-7.)

It is also easier and quicker for me to set my calipers because I can measure directly from the model. (See Illus. 9-8.) This is much faster than reading a written notation and then holding the calipers against a ruler to set these measurements.

My model turning can also be used in a way that is similar to the reverse template. When the model is held against the turning in the lathe, I can compare the symmetry of the various elements, much the way you can make a complete image by holding one half of a shape on the surface of a mirror. For example, two

Illus. 9-6. Laying out the squares simultaneously on a group of blanks is not really a way to duplicate turnings, but rather a way to speed up the process.

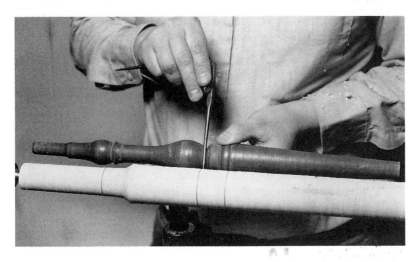

Illus. 9-7. Place a model leg against the spinning blank to transfer the critical points. Lightly scratch these points into the surface with a divider leg.

Illus. 9-8. Transfer the diameters from the model with a pair of calipers.

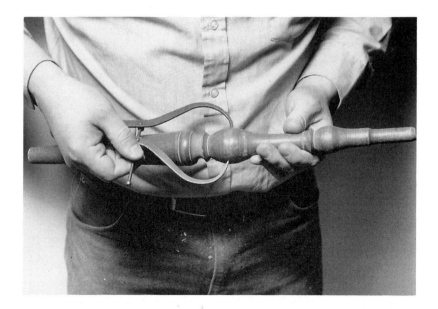

Illus. 9-9. The model turning technique is effective in that it is hard to find discrepancies, even when the turnings are laid side by side for comparison.

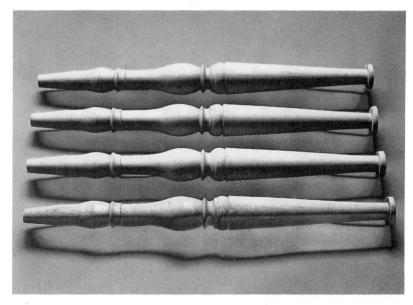

coves side by side (one on the model, the other on the work) will read as mirror images of each other, and their symmetry can be easily compared.

The space between the two turnings is itself a two-sided image whose symmetry can be inspected for discrepancies. Look at the four turnings shown in Illus. 9-9. They have been laid side by side so that you can better see the symmetrical image created by their two profiles.

It is not necessary to turn off the lathe to compare the model to the turning you are

making, unless the part includes square sections. In this case, the lathe needs to be turned off so that the revolving square does not knock against the stationary one, damaging one or both of them.

When you are done with a project, store the model part (or models, if there is more than one) for future reference. Keep it with any other models you have made. If you ever have to make any of those parts again, their models will quickly give you all the information needed.

10
TURNING GREEN WOOD

A lot has been written over the past decade about working green wood, especially about the techniques for turning this material. Green wood is unseasoned wood, direct from the log. It still contains much of the water and sap that sustained the living tree.

Today's woodworkers usually buy their material directly from a lumber dealer, and the first time they see it, it is already finished boards, complete with planed surfaces and square edges. However, all the wood you use in your woodworking started out green, and had to be processed through a number of stages by a number of different people. First, the living trees were cut down, and their trunks sawed. Then the wood was dried either through natural evaporation (called seasoning), or was forced-dried. Finally it was graded, dimensioned, bundled, and shipped to your lumber dealer, who sold it to you.

Working green wood is a very different experience from that just described in that it requires you to become involved with the earliest stages of processing wood into usable stock. The sawyer, wholesaler, and retailer no longer stand between you and the freshly cut log. Because you do most of this work yourself, your association with the wood is much more intimate, and, as a result, you come to think about the material in very different ways. You also learn a lot more about wood.

When bowl turners use green wood, they often use a chain saw to cut the blocks they need. However, there is a better method for obtaining turning blanks that are useful for making furniture and building parts. It is called riving. Riving is a process of controlled splitting. It is an ancient technique, and for millennia was used by woodworkers to obtain lathe blanks and even short boards. Until the late 17th century, when water-driven saw mills

became common, most plank was hand-sawn by teams of pit sawyers. Hand sawing was a labor-intensive process, and the lumber made this way was very expensive. To avoid this cost, much of the wood used in furniture and in building construction was riven directly from the log. (See Illus. 10-1.)

As late as the mid-19th century, chairmakers in the United States still rived the wood they used for chair parts. (See Illus. 10-2.) Well into this century, British bodgers (itinerant turners) moved from forest to forest, cutting down trees, bucking the trunks into billets, and riving the billets into turning blanks.

Many woodworkers still rive their turning

Illus. 10-1. The small oak boards used to make this candle box were riven directly from the log.

Illus. 10-2. The blemishes on the cylinders and beads of this "sausage and ring" ladder-back chair are tearout that occurred when the wood was rived. The blank was not thick enough for a complete leg, but the chairmaker turned it anyway.

freshly fallen log, there are alternatives. Perhaps you can buy your logs directly from loggers, or buy them from saw mills. Both businesses can be located through the telephone directory. However, you may have to drive out into the country to pick up your log, as they may not want to deliver it.

Even though I live in a city, logs are always readily available to me, and are dropped off in my driveway. I buy them from the same fellow who sells me my stove wood. He was always delighted to sell me whole logs, as he charges me the same amount as for wood he has had to cut and split.

Even if you are not a chairmaker and want to only occasionally use turnings in your work, you can still find suitable material in the pile of firewood you use to heat your stove or fireplace. Examine your cordwood (I am assuming that it is unseasoned) as you stack it. You will always find straight-grained pieces that can be rived into turning blanks. You will also find wood with exotic figures, such as curly maple. The only problem with cutting turning stock from stove wood is that, depending on the length of wood you burn, you are limited to 16- to 24-inch blanks.

There are reasons other than saving money that make it worthwhile to use riven wood. Riven wood is usually stronger than sawn turning squares. A saw will cut across the grain as easily as along it.

If the grain runs out of the turning square, the part you make from it will be weak at the point of run out. (See Illus. 10-3.) Just consider how many times you have had to glue a chair part that has broken at an angle. It broke at the area where the grain ran out of the part. (See Illus. 10-4.)

This type of break does not happen to parts made from riven wood. The splitting process follows the wood's grain, so that most of the fibres in a riven blank run continuously from one end to the other. In fact, in many species you can pull off a uniform strip of wood that's

stock, in part to save money. Riven wood is the least costly wood you will ever use. After all, you provide all the labor and equipment needed to make the turning blanks.

The money saved from using riven blanks is especially important to craftsmen who do a lot of turning. For example, sixty percent of the parts in a Windsor chair are turned. The chairmaker who uses riven blanks rather than sawn turning squares saves the difference in the cost of the materials.

Using riven wood is most easy for people who own a wood lot, or who have access to one. If you live in a large city where you cannot readily cut down a tree or easily purchase a

Illus. 10-3. If the grain runs out of a turning square, the part you make from it will be weak.

Illus. 10-4. A part is weak where the grain runs out of it. When it breaks, the split will follow the grain.

the thickness of a toothpick and as long as the blank. (See Illus. 10-5.) Because the grain runs continuously from one end of the turning to the other, the wood is stronger and more flexible. It can only fail by breaking at a right angle across the fibres. This is called shearing across the grain. (See Illus. 10-6.) This extra strength is important in many applications. Once again, take the example of turned chairmaking. Riven wood allows you to make parts that are more delicate without worrying that they are too weak to support a sitter's weight.

Also, riven wood is much more stable than sawn blanks. It is also less prone to check cracks, warping, and twisting. These qualities are also partially attributable to the straight grain. However, they can also be attributed to the fact that a riven turning blank represents a radial section. A radial section results when a pie-shaped piece is cut from a log. Radially sawn clapboards (prized by carpenters for their stability) are the most commonly known example of this type of cut. Illus. 10-7 shows the unique grain pattern that occurs in a radially sawn clapboard and gives it its legendary stability.

To better understand why a riven blank is a radial section, consider how the splitting is done. The log is halved and quartered. Each quarter is then split into eighths, resulting in a wedge-shaped cross section just like that of a slice of pie. Depending on the diameter of the log, each eighth will render three blanks, as shown in Illus. 10-8. Note how the end grain runs almost in straight lines through each blank, just as it does in clapboard. If you were to turn a part from a blank while it is still green, it will not warp or check as it dries. Instead, it will become oval in cross section.

All of the recent emphasis on working green wood might lead you to think that your goal is to obtain unseasoned wood. However, if you

Illus. 10-5. The grain in a riven blank runs uninterrupted from one end to the other. It is possible to pull off strips as thin as a toothpick and as long as the blank.

Illus. 10-6. Because of its continuous grain, riven wood is generally much stronger than that which is sawn. When a riven part breaks, it will shear across the grain.

Illus. 10-7. The end grain of a riven, birch turning blank and a pine clapboard show that they both contain a radial section. This makes them very stable.

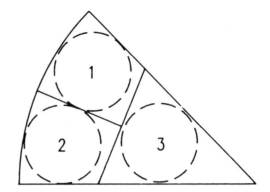

Illus. 10-8. When the three turning blanks are laid out like this, you can usually rive them from ⅛th of a billet.

consider all the reasons that have been given for using riven turning blanks, you will notice that none of them have anything to do with the wood being green. Logs are riven because this process yields inexpensive wood that is stronger and more stable than sawn turning squares. You have to start with a freshly cut log, not so you can obtain green wood, but for the same reason that boards are sawn from green logs—if left in the log, the wood will decay. The log has to be sawn or rived so the wood can dry without rotting.

For most turning applications, riven wood has to be seasoned before it can be used. (Methods of seasoning riven turning blanks are discussed below.) While it is possible to turn freshly rived wood, it is so wet it "spits." The sap causes rust spots on both the lathe and your tools. Although very sharp turning tools will cut green wood like a hot knife cuts butter, it is impossible to create glassy, smooth surfaces in the soft, wet wood. It is equally difficult to make crisp details.

As was discussed in Chapter 6, different species of woods have different properties that make some more suitable for making turned parts than others. So, some species of wood rive better than do others. The wood you are using should cleave cleanly—that is, separate after only several blows, resulting in a split with smooth sides. You do not want to use a stringy wood, because one side will tear strands of wood out of the other. In a worst case scenario, the tearing will be so bad that you will have to reach into the split with a hatchet and snip the wood pulled from the two sides. This type of damage to the sides of a split will require you to rive larger blanks, to ensure that the blank contains sufficient undamaged wood to yield a turning. On the other hand, woods that rive cleanly allow you to split blanks very near the dimension of the intended turning.

I do not have a working knowledge of all American woods, and cannot advise you as to which rive well. It's recommended that you experiment with the specific species you are interested in. I can relate my experiences with American eastern hardwoods. Red and silver maple, American beech, and white (paper) birch are evenly textured woods that split very well. Hard (sugar) maple, and black (sweet) and yellow birch are all evenly textured, but tear. Black cherry tears the most. Of the ring porous woods, red oak, white ash, and hickory split very easily. White oak is stringy, and tears.

When riving, you can feel and hear the difference between wood that splits cleanly and one that tears. Species that rive well make a distinct "pop" when they release. Stringy woods that pull strands from each side of the split make a tearing sound.

Though a particular species of wood can be riven easily, the quality should not supersede the concerns described in Chapter 6. You still need to choose a wood for its turning properties, not for its riving qualities. For example, if you are making baluster turnings that have crisp elements that are distinctly defined and differentiated, do not use red oak simply because it rives well.

Though some species of wood rive better than others, not every log of that particular species is suitable for riving. The log you choose should not contain any live knots (knots that were living limbs when the tree was felled) or any encased knots (dead limbs that broke off and have since been covered by later growth). Wherever either of the two flaws occur in a log, the grain will be deflected around them. Not only will the wood be very hard to rive (for the same reason, it is hard to split stove

wood with knots), the blanks you obtain will usually be too twisted and bent to make a turning. For this reason, be selective when choosing a log. Carefully examine it for defects. Other flaws you should look for include wind shakes, twisted or spiral growth, and decay.

A collection of tools is needed for riving. (See Illus. 10-9.) Unfortunately, they are not tools you are likely to use in the woodworking you do at the bench. You should have a six-pound splitting maul (eight pounds is too heavy), a pair of steel wedges, a wooden club called a beetle (this tool can itself be made on a lathe), and a froe or a Kent hatchet (one with a wide, thin blade). A tape measure is also needed.

A chain saw will quickly buck the log into lengths, which are called billets. You can also do this by hand, using either a bucksaw or a large (36-inch) tubular metal brush saw. Both of these saws take more work to use than a chain saw, and require more time. However, if you rive infrequently, they are a less-expensive alternative.

Using the metal splitting wedges by driving

Illus. 10-9. A collection of riving tools. Counterclockwise from top, they are: a wooden maul (sometimes called a beetle), a Kent hatchet, a six-pound splitting *maul, a peavey (not essential, but handy for moving logs), and a pair of wedges.*

them in with the metal maul, first halve and then quarter the billets. Split the blanks from the billets with either a froe or a Kent hatchet. Always drive both of these splitting tools with a beetle. Never use the splitting maul, because the force of metal against metal will eventually destroy the froe or the Kent hatchet.

Before bucking a log, examine it for blemishes such as live or encased knots. If possible, cut the billets from between the blemishes. Buck the billets a couple of inches longer than the finished blanks you need for turning. As the blank seasons, its end grain will collapse, case-harden, and perhaps develop small checks. Thus, the ends of the blank have to be trimmed before it can be safely turned. Before placing a seasoned blank in the lathe, cut at least ½ inch off either end with a small (21-inch) brush saw.

Before riving the billets into turning blanks, remember that it is a controlled process. It is not like splitting firewood, where the blow has to be strong, but not necessarily well placed. Instead, work more slowly and more deliberately. After every few blows, stop to determine your progress.

Turn the billet on one end and halve it using two splitting wedges and the maul. Set the wedges on either side of the pith so that the wedges and pith form a straight line. Also use the maul and wedges to quarter and eighth the halves. (See Illus. 10-10.)

Next, use a soft lead pencil or a piece of chalk to sketch out the finished blanks on the end grain. (After some experience, you will be able to skip this step.) Use either a froe or a Kent hatchet to rive out the rough blanks. (See Illus. 10-11.)

After all the billets have been rived into rough blanks, take them into the shop. Use a large drawknife to peel off the bark and shave the green blanks to their rough-round dimensions. (See Illus. 10-12.) Do not try to shave the blanks to their final diameter. Instead, they should be left slightly large for reasons that will be explained below.

Stack the blanks where they can dry. They should be raised off the ground (or floor) on a platform such as a pallet. The blanks should also be exposed on both ends, as that is where most of the evaporation takes place. If they are stored outside, they should be protected from rain.

Depending on the drying conditions, the blanks will season sufficiently so they can be turned into furniture or building parts in about 6–12 months. You can use them sooner than that, but you risk encountering problems such as joints loosening due to tenon shrinkage. When I made Windsor chairs, I avoided any such difficulties by leaving the newly turned parts in a warm (175°F) oven for most of a day. This temperature dries the wood completely, but is low enough that it does not cause honeycombing (internal checking).

Because riven turning blanks are irregular(merely rough-rounded with a drawknife) they are best used for parts that do not have

Illus. 10-10. This white birch billet has been halved, quartered, and eighthed with splitting wedges driven by a maul.

Illus. 10-11. The eighths are rived into turning blanks with a Kent hatchet driven with an oak maul. The oak maul was itself turned from a large, riven blank.

Illus. 10-12. The blanks are rough-rounded with a drawknife and stacked to dry.

square sections. That is why riven wood is most commonly used in turned chairmaking (Windsors and ladder-backs).

Still, it is possible to make riven blanks into turning squares. Plane a flat surface on the blank with a hand plane, and hold this face against the fence of a jointer. This will allow you to joint a second surface that is square with the first. Turn the blank end-over-end and square the third and fourth sides. However, unless for some reason you need the superior strength of riven wood, it is a lot easier to saw turning squares from plank.

Chucking a riven blank in the lathe is not as easy to do as with turning squares. You cannot locate the center of the blank by merely making an X on the end grain. If the piece is perfectly straight and of a uniform thickness, try locating the center points by eye. When the piece is chucked, turn on the lathe. You will see an image with blurred outer edges and a solid center. This solid area should be of a uniform width from one end to the other. So should the blurred edges. Also, the lathe should not be vibrating much more than if you had chucked up a turning square. If it is, look to see where the unevenness is occurring. You should be able to see the eccentricity in both the blurred edge and the solid center. Shut off the lathe and loosen the tail center so that the billet will spin freely on the two center points (so that the spurs are not engaging the end). Gravity will pull the off-center mass downward. To better balance the billet, relocate one (or both) centers so the billet spins more smoothly and evenly.

When rough-rounding green wood, you will not hear the uniform staccato knock a square edge makes against the roughing gouge. Instead, as the gouge passes along the blank, it cuts through an irregular surface, so that some places along the length will strike against the tool with more force than others. However, all you have to do is make several passes back and forth along the blank to quickly bring the surface close to round. From this point on, the techniques for turning green wood are the same as for turning squares.

11
OFF-CENTER TURNINGS

The cabriole leg is well-known to all furniture makers who do reproductions. It is closely associated with the Queen Anne and Chippendale styles where it was used on tables, chairs, beds, desks, and chests of drawers. The Queen Anne cabriole leg typically terminates in a pad foot (less frequently, either a slipper or a trifid foot), while the Chippendale leg ends in a claw and ball foot. (See Illus. 11-1 and 11-2.)

Both types of cabriole leg are cut out of solid plank with either a band or a bow saw. The rough legs are then shaped and carved by hand. All this work is timeconsuming and labor-intensive, and, as a result, cabriole legs are used only on expensive formal furniture.

However, similar types of legs can be made much more quickly in the lathe using a technique called off-center turning. This process is accomplished by moving the tail-stock center between two different locations on the end of the turning blank. The result is a leg that appears to be offset in the same way that a true cabriole leg is.

During the 18th century, these simulated cabriole legs were generally used on country and informal (utilitarian) Queen Anne furniture. (See Illus. 11-3.) However, they were also used on some high-style pieces such as tables and desks. (See Illus. 11-4.)

The pad-footed, trumpet-shaped legs of turned Hudson River Valley chairs, popular in eastern New York state during the late 18th century, were also made from off-center turnings. Another off-center turned leg, called a Duck Foot, was used on some informal Chippendale chairs.

These off-center-turned, simulated cabriole legs fell out of favor shortly before the end of the 18th century, when the real cabriole leg ceased to be fashionable.

If you are making reproductions, you, too, can use off-center turnings for the same purpose as early furniture makers—to create simulated cabriole legs that appear to be elaborately shaped—while taking advantage of the lathe's speed and accuracy. However, you can also use off-center turnings on furniture you have designed yourself.

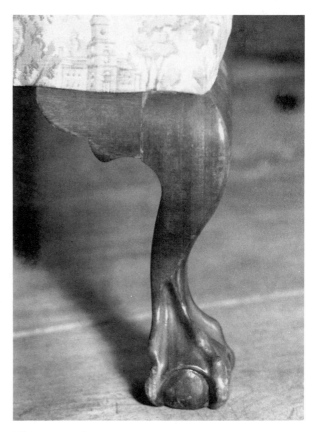

Illus. 11-1. There are two types of cabriole leg. The first is the claw and ball legs that are associated with the Chippendale style of furniture making.

Illus. 11-2. The second type of cab-riole leg is used on Queen Anne furniture, such as this lowboy.

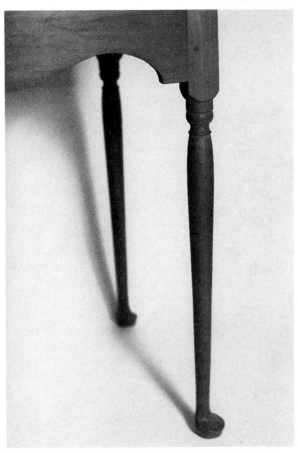

Illus. 11-3. Simulated cabriole legs like the ones shown on this utilitarian tavern table can be turned in the lathe.

Illus. 11-4. Simulated cabriole legs were also used on very sophisticated furniture. This mahogany corner chair has a shaped cabriole leg, as well as three that are turned.

Begin with a turning blank that is as long as the finished leg. If you are making Hudson River Valley chairs, you can use a riven blank. However, most commonly, you will need to start with a turning square. Locate the centers by making an X on each end of the blank. Chuck the piece in the lathe using these centers. Use a try square and a soft lead pencil to lay out the square section at the top of the leg, where the skirt will be joined. (I usually place the top of the leg towards the headstock.)

Turn on the lathe and separate the square section with a plunge cut made with a parting tool. (See Illus. 11-5.) If you want to round the lower corners, do so now by making a rolling cut with a skew. If you plan to leave the corner square, face it off with a skew or a diamond point. Both cuts are explained in Chapter 6.

Next, use a gouge to round the foot (usually the tail-stock end), to the blank's maximum diameter. This round section should extend about three inches up the blank. (See Illus. 11-6.)

Shut off the lathe and retract the tail-stock's center from the end of the blank. Relocate the center about halfway along one of the X lines (it does not matter which one) and retighten the tail stock. (See Illus. 11-7.)

Because the turning is now off center and quite eccentric, it will be necessary to relocate the rest. Before switching the lathe back on, spin the wood by hand to make sure that it will clear the rest. If not, the eccentric blank will spin into the rest with sufficient force to possi-

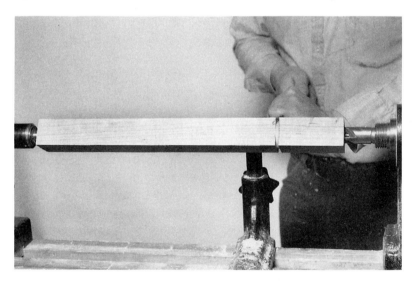

Illus. 11-5. Lay out the square where the rails will be joined to the leg. Do this with a parting tool.

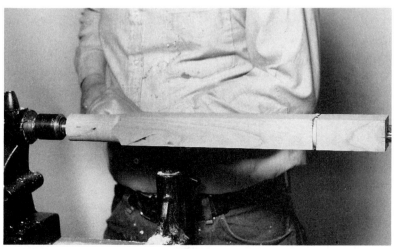

Illus. 11-6. Next, round the foot end to the blank's maximum diameter

Illus. 11-7. Find a second center about halfway along one of the lines of the X.

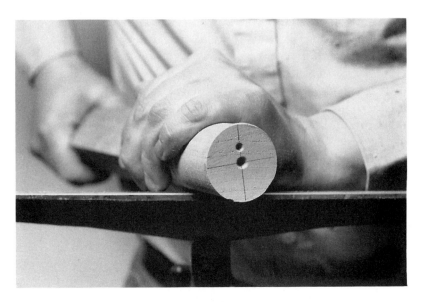

bly damage itself. The off-center blank will also be out of balance, and cause the lathe to vibrate.

When you turn on the machine, keep your hands and tools out of the way until you have had a chance to look through the blur and determine the outline of the blank's swing. Also, take note of the limits of the swing before you advance the gouge into the eccentric blank. Otherwise, you might take too heavy a cut, which could stall the lathe or even break a piece of wood out of one corner of the blank.

Use a roughing gouge to round the area between the square section at the top of the leg and the foot. Because this area is eccentric, rough-rounding it will quickly reduce the amount of vibration. Because the foot is off-center, rounding the long area between the square and the foot will result in a long taper. It will be thickest just under the square, and will steadily narrow to form the leg's ankle. If you look through the blur, you can see in advance the shape of the taper you will be making. (See Illus. 11-8.)

Next, smooth the upper surface of the foot, with a ¼-inch spindle gouge using the technique described below. (See Illus. 11-9.) The foot area of the blank is the most off-center and, as a result, it is in contact with the gouge for less than half of each revolution. Each turn of the blank knocks the top of the foot against

the gouge, and unless you maintain a steady hand, it is easy to mar this surface. The top of the foot is the most visible surface of the leg, and a mistake here will be very obvious to anyone who sees your work.

To cut the top of the foot, roll the gouge on its side as you would if making a cove. (See Chapter 7.) In fact, what you are actually doing is making one half of a steep-sided cove.

Grip the gouge tightly and steadily. Slowly advance it, making sure that the bezel stays in a path that will keep it in contact with the top of the foot. This is not easy, as the foot is in contact with the gouge only part of the time. As the gouge works down the surface of foot, roll it so it follows the curve that blends the foot into the ankle. This is an important step, because it removes all evidence of the two processes used to make the turning.

Shut off the lathe and look at the foot's upper surface to determine if it has been smoothly cut. Not only is this area the most eccentric part of the turning, it is also the area where the end grain is. Therefore, some sanding is always required. However, the less digging and scoring you do, the easier this cleanup will be.

With a skew, plane the tapered leg to remove any gouge marks. Start the planing just below the square and work down as close to the foot as possible.

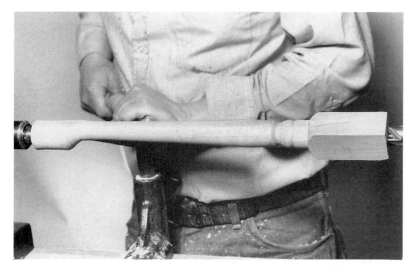

Illus. 11-8. Turn the eccentric leg to round and shape the ankle.

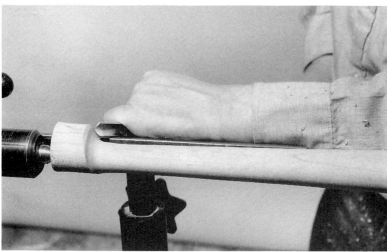

Illus. 11-9. Smooth the upper surface of the foot with a ¼-inch spindle gouge. This technique is very much like the method used to shape one side of a cove.

Next, shut off the lathe. Retract the tail stock and remount the leg on the original center. Now, when you start the lathe, it is the foot that will be turning true, and the leg that is eccentric.

Form the pad (the thin, round platform on which the foot stands) by making a plunge cut with a ¼-inch skew. (See Illus. 11-10.) Unless you are copying another leg, the pad has no set diameter, so practice and determine the diameter you prefer.

Round the bottom edge (the toe) of the foot by making a rolling cut with a skew. (See Illus. 11-11.) The length of the radius you use to round the edge is, once again, determined by how you want the foot to appear. A long radius will make the toe very thin and pointed, while a short radius will leave it blunt and robust. (See Illus. 11-12.)

There are fewer design possibilities available to you when making these simulated cabriole legs than when making real cabriole legs. The only other way to design a simulated cabriole leg that has not been mentioned is to increase or decrease the distance between the foot's two centers. This will vary the thickness of the ankle, which inversely alters the width of the foot. In other words, a thin ankle results in a wide foot, while a thick ankle results in a narrow foot.

The thickness of the ankle usually depends on the piece of furniture you are making. (See Chapter 8.) A slender ankle is very appealing on a light, delicate form like a tea table. For

Illus. 11-10. Mount the leg back on its original center and form the pad by making a plunge cut with a ¼-inch skew.

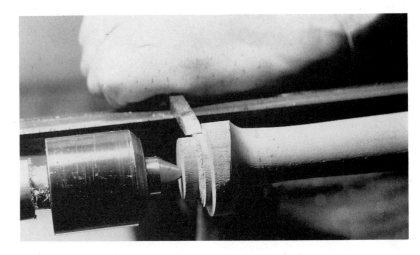

Illus. 11-11. Round the toe by making a rolling cut with a skew.

Illus. 11-12. When making a cabriole leg's toe, you can produce different results if you vary the length of the radius. A long radius, as shown at A, creates a fine, delicate toe. A short radius, as shown at B, makes the toe robust and blunt.

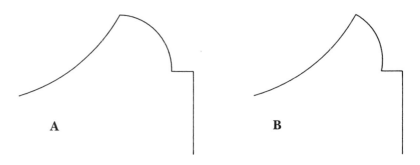

A   B

heavier furniture, such as a desk, the ankle has to be more substantial.

One word of caution: A simulated cabriole leg is turned on two centers, with the foot aligned with one corner of the square. (Remember, you located the off center on one of the diagonal lines of the X used to mark the blank's center.) As a result, the actual leg is cocked slightly rearwards towards the diagonally opposite corner. Normally this misalignment is not noticeable. In fact, your eyes see the foot as actually projecting forward, as on a genuine cabriole leg.

This illusion works as long as the legs are a

reasonable distance apart. However, should you use these off-center turned legs on a small piece such as a stand, a problem arises. When the distance between the legs is short, the misalignment becomes more apparent, and the piece appears to have bowed legs that are cocked diagonally inward. This makes the piece look like it is slowly buckling under a massive, unseen weight.

Always be sure that you locate the center of the tail stock on one of the lines of the X you made to locate the blank's center. This ensures that the toe is placed below one corner of the square section where the skirt is joined to the cabriole leg. In the finished piece of furniture, all four toes will then be catercornered (in a diagonal or oblique position).

If you are designing furniture rather than reproducing a period piece, you may want the foot to point forward, rearwards, or to one side. To do this, locate the second center at the midpoint between two lines of the X. The only historical precedent I know of for placing the off center in this manner is the Egyptian-inspired lion's paw legs used on some early Empire furniture.

12

REEDS AND FLUTES

Reeds and flutes are very similar vertical decorative elements that are often added to turnings to create texture on the turning's surface. Because both reeds and flutes run in the direction of the turning's axis, they act as lines that help move the viewer's eye along that line of axis. In other words, when used on a vertical part, they give the part visual appeal by reinforcing the verticality.

Both reeds and flutes are usually made in the lathe, but not while the machine is running. Instead, use the lathe's centers as a vise to hold the turning stationary while you work on it.

The major difference between reeds and flutes is that reeds are convex, while flutes are concave. Also, flutes are usually carved into the surface of either a cylinder or a very gradual taper. They are not usually carved on a vase or an urn (although there is no technical reason why they cannot be). Reeds, on the other hand, frequently decorate the surfaces of all four shapes.

Reeds and flutes were developed by the classical Greeks and Romans, and were used to decorate architectural elements such as the shafts of temple columns and pilasters. Because they were first developed in the classical periods, they are also closely associated with the neo-classicism of the late 18th and early 19th centuries, a time that is known in America as the Federal period and in England as Adam and George III. There was also another less well-known revival of classicism during the early 20th century, when both reeds and flutes again became popular.

In architecture, reeds and flutes are still used the way the Greeks originally intended: to decorate columns and pilasters. However, they are also included on such elements as stair balusters, newel posts, balustrades (widow's walks), and porches and fence posts.

Reeds and flutes are used on furniture as well as in architecture. (See Illus. 12-1–12-15.) In fact, reeds are the feature most closely associated with furniture made in the Sheraton style (along with Adam and Hepplewhite, Sheraton is one of the styles that make up the neo-classical period).

Reeds and flutes have also been used in other periods to decorate vertical elements such as table legs, pedestals, chair legs, arm stumps, and bedposts.

Since both reeds and flutes run vertically (along the axis of the part), they cannot be made by turning, and have to be carved separately. They can both be made with a router, and, in fact, that is the method most often used. However using the router requires you to build elaborate jigs and fixtures and to set up the machine every time you want to make reeds or flutes.

Making reeds or flutes by hand is much simpler, and—unless you are making large numbers of the same part—also often faster.

To make reeds and flutes, you first have to lay them out. One way is to use the center locator shown in Illus. 12-16. A center locator is essentially an upright post held in a flat base. The lower horizontal piece is placed on the lathe bed and slides back and forth on this surface. The vertical post grips a soft lead pencil, and can be adjusted up or down by the loosening of a bolt. This allows you to set the pencil point at exactly the height of the lathe's two centers.

Illus. 12-1. Both reeds and flutes are closely associated with neo-classical furniture and architecture. However, both have been widely used in other periods and can be incorporated into your own designs. Reeds are a design element on the needed urn on a tripod stand shown here. See Illus. 12-2–12-5 for more examples.

Illus. 12-2. The leg on a Sheraton-period sofa.

Illus. 12-3. Sheraton-period bedposts.

Illus. 12-4. The stump on a Sheraton-period sofa.

Illus. 12-5. The spindles on the back of a Sheraton-period settee.

Illus. 12-6–12-9. Flutes are a part of the design of this Chippendale-period bedpost and the pieces shown in 12-7–12-9.

Illus. 12-7. The leg/stile of a Louis XVI fauteuil.

Illus. 12-8. The stretcher of a side table.

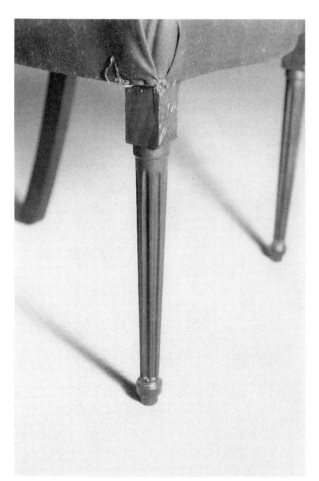

Illus. 12-9. The leg of a Sheraton-period chair.

Illus. 12-10—12-15. Examples of architectural reeding and fluting. Shown here is a Victorian newel post.

Illus. 12-11. A column on a Victorian mantel piece.

Illus. 12-12. A Victorian porch column.

Illus. 12-13. A Georgian newel and balusters.

Illus. 12-14. An urn on a Federal fence.

Illus. 12-15. A column on a Federal mantelpiece.

dle. It is divided into a number of segments that the manufacturer determines to be the most useful, usually an even number. Index heads commonly come in segments of 12, 24, or 60. Marking each segment is a hole, or a punched dimple. Also attached to the headstock is a lock that when slid into the hole secures the headstock so that it cannot be turned. The lock can simply be a steel rod that slips through the holes.

The number of holes included in the index head allow you to easily divide the turning into horizontal segments. For example, index heads with 12, 24, or 60 segments divide in half, as well as in quarters, sixths, twelfths, etc.

To illustrate how an index head is used, assume that your lathe has a 24-hole disc and that you want to lay out a turning with 12 reeds. Secure the head by sliding the lock through any hole (it does not matter which), and trace a line using the center locator. This has created a starting point from which you will now work. Release the lock and rotate the index head two holes. It does not matter in which direction you turn it. Slide in the lock and trace another line. Repeat the process 10

Making the center locator is a simple task for any woodworker with experience on the bench. Drill a 9/32-inch hole in the post. This hole will hold the pencil. You can easily remove the pencil to sharpen it. Use a #2 lead pencil, as this is soft enough to leave a dark line that can be easily seen.

To use the center locator, place the device on the bed at one end of the area to be reeded (or fluted) and push the pointed end of the pencil against the turning. Slide the center locator along the turning, keeping the pencil tip in contact with the wood. It will trace a clear line, exactly at the height of the turning's axis, even when the line is traced over an element that constantly changes diameter, such as a vase.

An index head (see Chapter 1) is another device that is handy (although not required) when you are making reeds or flutes. An index head is a disc attached to the headstock spin-

Illus. 12-16. A cluster of 12 reeds can be easily laid out with a 24-hole index head. Simply skip every other hole.

more times, skipping one hole each time you turn the index head. This will bring you back to the starting point, and you will have divided the turning into 12 perfectly equal segments. (See Illus. 12-16.)

If your lathe does not have an index head, you can still divide a turning into segments by walking them off with a pair of dividers. Determine how many segments you need and set the dividers to roughly the reed's thickness. Make a starting point on the turning so you know when you have made a complete revolution. Walk the dividers around the turning's diameter, keeping count. You may have to adjust the dividers a couple of times to ensure that the segments come out even. When they do, walk off the segments a final time while making a pencil mark at each place where the divider points touch the wood. (See Illus. 12-17.) Each time you use the center locator, place the pencil point on one of these marks and trace a line.

You can lay out six and 12 reeds very easily if you remember that the radius of a circle will divide the diameter of a turning into six segments. Obviously, half the radius will result in 12 segments. The radius of your turning is the distance from the center to the outside edge. You can also measure the turning with a pair of calipers and divide this measurement in half to find the radius.

One final decorative detail you should be familiar with is called a stop flute. A stop flute is a flute with a reed in the bottom third (approximately) of its length. Stop flutes are laid out in the same process used for reeding, but, like fluting, are usually only used on cylinders or very gradual tapers.

Making Reeds

There are two kinds of reeds. The first type, called a straight reed, is made with a plane rather than being carved, so it is by far the easier of the two to make. However, this type of reed can only be used in certain applications. Because it is made with a plane, it is of a constant width. Thus, this reed can only be used on cylinders or very gradual tapers. Also, the ends of the reeds have to be exposed, or open, and cannot terminate at a projecting detail such as an astragal. (See Illus. 12-18.)

You can use one of two types of planes to make a straight reed. (See Illus. 12-19.) The first is a very common wooden moulding plane called a center bead. Although center beads are not being made any more, they are readily available from antique tool dealers. Many of these shops sell their merchandise through the mail, so center beads are available to you no matter wherever you are located.

The other plane that can be used is a combination plane. The best known of these is the

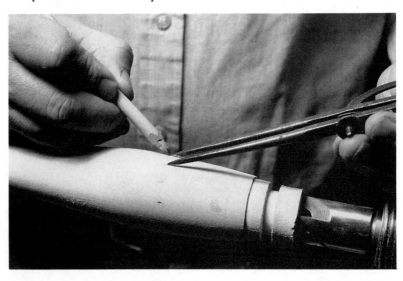

Illus. 12-17. Reeds can also be walked-off with a pair of dividers.

Illus. 12-18. The straight reeds on this Sheraton bureau were made with a center bead plane. The cap, colloquially called a "cookie corner," was applied later. Otherwise, both ends of the reeds are open.

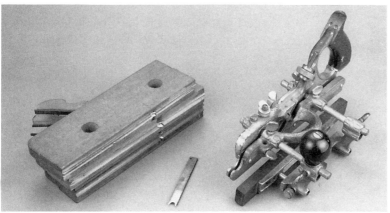

Illus. 12-19. To make straight reeds, you can either use a wooden center bead (three of them are shown here stacked together) or a combination plane such as the well-known Stanley #45. A hollow cutter for the #45 lies between the planes.

Stanley #45 (See Illus. 12-19.) Although this tool is not being made anymore either, it is easy to find one. Furthermore, reproductions of #45s are still being made, although they are sold under different names. Other types of combination planes are also available. These planes are sometimes called multiplanes. Multiplanes and reproductions of #45s can be purchased through just about all of the numerous direct-mail tool catalogues available.

Wooden center bead planes come in different sizes. Each plane makes just one width of reed. If you own just one plane (or a couple), you will be limited to the width of reeds you can make. Combination planes come with a selection of interchangeable bead cutters (as well as a variety of other shapes) of different widths. Choose the size reed you need and adjust the plane's sliding section to that cutter.

One other consideration: the bottom edges of the cutters must end in points so that they produce a V groove rather than a flat-bottomed cut (known as a quirk). If the ends of the cutter are square (so that they make quirks), the reeds will be undercut and damaged. In this case, you have to grind the edges of your center bead's cutter to create points. Do the same to your combination plane's cutters if they have square ends. (See Illus. 12-20.)

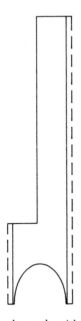

Illus. 12-20. To make reeds with a combination plane, you have to grind the cutter to create sharp points instead of square ends.

After you have shaped the part, unplug the lathe motor so that it cannot start accidentally. Lock the index head, and, using the center locator, trace a line along the cylinder. This reeding process is somewhat automatic and, as a result, this is the only line you will need to make. Use a small carver's V parting tool to cut a narrow V groove along the line. (See Illus. 12-21).

Next, use the plane to make the reeds. A right-handed person will find it easiest to do this type of reeding from behind the lathe rather than from where he would stand when turning. Place one side of the center bead's sole (or the combination's plane's skate) in the V groove. Make the first pass of the plane slowly while watching one side of the sole in the V groove. The plane should cut the two bevelled grooves on either side of a reed. If necessary, make a second pass to fully form the reed.

Return the plane to the end of the section that is being reeded. Place the plane so that the far side of the sole rides in the nearest side of the reed just made. This will cause the plane to track parallel to the first reed while cutting the second.

Illus. 12-21. Begin making straight reeds by tracing a single line with the center locator. Score the line with a small carver's V parting tool.

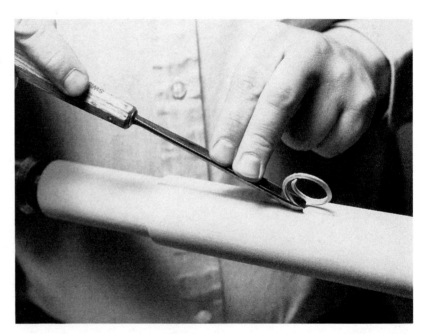

Illus. 12-22. Place one side of the plane's cutter in the V groove, and, tracking in the groove, run your first reed. Several passes will be necessary to form it completely. Set one side of the cutter in one side of the first reed, and cut a second. Repeat this process as far around the turning as necessary.

Make another pass or two to develop the second reed. Move the plane a second time so that, once again, the far side of the cutter is riding in the nearest groove. Cut the third reed in the same manner as the first two. (See Illus. 12-22.) Complete the reeding in the same way. If you need to do any clean up at the beginning or end of a reed, use a small parting tool.

Traditionally, the second method of reeding is most common on vases and urns. However, if you do your own designing, reeding can be used on any long element, a ball, a bobbin, or a taper. It can also be done on a square, but in this case a plane (see above) is most commonly used. In Illus. 12-23–12-26 I am shown reeding a vase. Note that a plane would not work here because as the reeds pass over the swelling of the vase's body and down onto the neck, they have to first widen and then narrow so that the same number can fit on the increasing and the then decreasing surface area. A plane can only cut a reed of a constant width, so this type of reeding must instead be carved by hand.

Do nothing until you have disconnected the plug on the lathe motor to eliminate the possibility of an accidental startup. Using the index head, divide the turning into as many segments as there are reeds, or walk them off with a pair of dividers. Both processes are described above. (See Illus. 12–23.)

After locking the index head, use a small parting tool to carve the reeds. Start at the line which is facing directly upwards. The cut made by the tool should change in depth and width as it moves over the vase's body up to the neck. It should be deepest and widest over the body, and shallow and narrow on the neck. (See Illus. 12-24.)

Illus. 12-23. Reeds on a vase need to be carved. Lay them out with a center locator. Note how the reeds widen and narrow as they pass over the vase's wide body and down the narrow neck.

Illus. 12-24. Follow one of the lines with a carver's V parting tool.

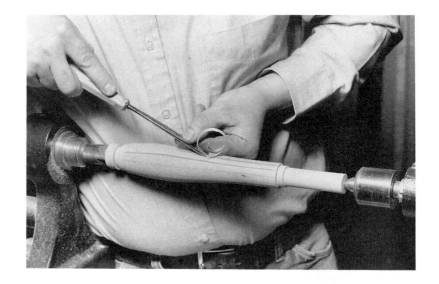

Illus. 12-25. Do the same on an adjacent line, and you will see the reed beginning to form. Continue all the way around the turning.

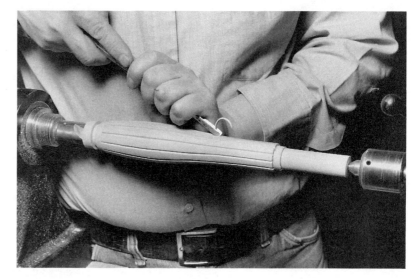

Illus. 12-26. The second time around the turning, roll the tool slightly to one side and trim the edge of the V groove. Do the same to the other side of the groove. Repeat this process all the way around the turning, and the reeds will become even more defined.

Release the lock on the index head and rotate the turning so the next line is facing up. Lock the index head and carve this second line in the same manner. Do the same for the remaining reeds. (See Illus. 12-25.)

Cutting the V grooves with a carver's parting tool has defined the reeds. Now you have to uniformly round them. Start this process with the same small parting tool. Roll the chisel lightly to the side so that one leg of the V-shaped cutting edge will trim the sharp arris of the adjoining reed. Be careful not to make too heavy a cut.

After following the reed all the way down the neck, return again to the beginning and place the parting tool in the same groove. This time, roll the chisel in the opposite direction and make the same type of cut on the edge of the other reed. These two steps have rounded the abutting edges of two adjacent reeds.

Move to the next groove and make the same two cuts, one on each side. Now one reed will have taken on a shape that approximates its final form. If you repeat these same two cuts in each groove all the way around the turning, all the reeds will be roughed out. (See Illus. 12-26.) Work completely around the turning rather than trying to finish each individual reed one at a time. Roughing them simul-

taneously helps establish consistency, which is essential, as the finished reeds will all have to be uniform in width.

Once you have made the two cuts in each groove and are back to the groove where you began, you can finish rounding the individual reeds. Use a flat carving chisel (¾-inch) for this work, the type of chisel with a bevel on both sides of the cutting edge. This tool will complete the rounding of the reeds. Do each one as close to its final form as possible. (See Illus. 12-27.)

If the reeds are closed (i.e., they stop at some other detail, such as a ring), clean up the corner formed at the end of the V groove with either a utility knife or a hobby knife. Use the pointed end of the blade to reach into the corner and snip any stray wood fibres.

Reeds often have a closed bottom and an open top. In this case, their tops are often rounded. This can be done very easily with a carving gouge. Hold the gouge vertically so that it makes a plunge cut. Turn the tool so that its bezel is facing upward, away from the reed. Push directly downward. This scores a round end, cleanly severing the wood fibres to the shape of the gouge's sweep. (See Illus. 12-28.) Remove the waste around the end with a flat chisel. (See Illus. 12-29.)

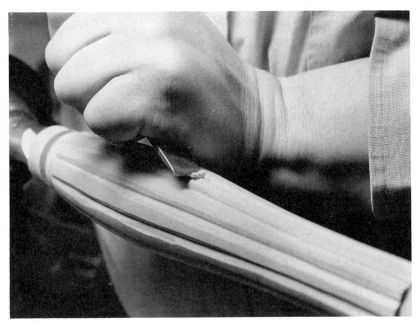

Illus. 12-27. Complete the reeds with a flat carver's chisel. Clean up with the corner of a scraper by sanding carefully.

Illus. 12-28. The ends of the reeds can be rounded. Make a plunge cut with a carving gouge of the desired width and sweep.

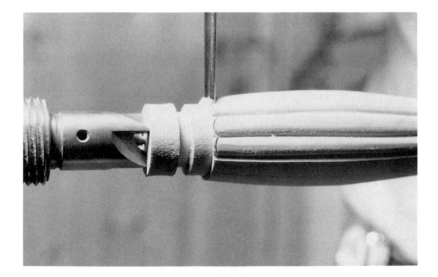

Illus. 12-29. Clean out the waste around the plunge cut with a chisel.

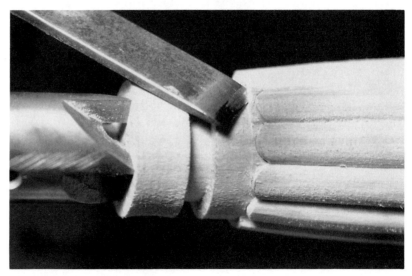

Making Flutes

Carved reeds butt against each other, but are separated by a V-groove. Flutes are separated in one of two different ways. There is a reason why. As mentioned, flutes originated as the decoration on the shafts of classical Grecian columns. Grecian architecture is divided into orders; fluting varies from order to order. In the Doric order, the flutes are separated by a pointed ridge called an arris. These type of flutes are called "arris flutes." There are normally 20 flutes on a Doric column.

On the shafts of Ionic and Corinthian columns, flutes are separated by a narrow strip of the shaft's original surface, called a fillet. These type of flutes are called "fillet flutes." On Ionic and Corinthian columns, there are normally 24 fillet flutes. Each fillet is half the width of a flute. The flutes are channelled into the shaft to a depth equal to half their width.*

If you are making arris flutes, lay them out

*This information, and further information about reeds and flutes, can be found in Asher Benjamin's *The Practical House Carpenter*, which is listed in the Bibliography on page 187.

the same way you would lay reeds out, using the center locator to divide the turning into equal segments. However, if you are instead separating the flutes with a fillet (as on the Ionic and Corinthian columns), the process is slightly more complicated.

Remember, you will typically want to make the fillet half the width of a flute. (Though this rule only applies to the Ionic and Corinthian order, and you can actually make your fillets as wide or narrow as you wish, I will assume that generally you will want to follow this ratio.) To do this, first determine how many index-head-holes-wide each flute will be and use half that number for each fillet. (See Illus. 12-30.) For example, if a flute is two holes wide, make each fillet one hole wide. If the flute is four holes wide, each fillet will be two holes wide.

Next, trace a starting line with the center locator and rotate the turning the width of one flute. Trace a second line. Next, rotate the turning the width of one fillet (half a flute), and trace another line. Complete this process all the way around. Doing this has divided the turning into a series of segments that alternate: wide, narrow, wide, narrow, etc.

As with reeds, flutes can be made in two ways. The first method is also done with a plane, which is again only possible when the flutes are open at both ends. The wooden version of the plane you need is called a round. A round is a moulding plane with a convex-curved sole. A round plane is part of a pair of planes. Its mate is a concave-soled plane called a hollow. Each pair of hollows and rounds is part of a graduated set of 9 pairs (18 planes) of different radii.

You do not need to own a complete set of hollows and rounds to make flutes. You only have to have the one or two sizes that make the width of the flute you are using. If you are fluting porch columns, you will need much larger sizes of rounds than if you are fluting table legs.

You can also use a combination plane to make flutes. These planes also come with a set of round cutters (just as they have a set of center reed cutters). You only need to select the radius required for the fluting you are doing. (See Illus. 12-31.)

To make flutes, first cut a shallow channel with a carving gouge. Next, lay the sole of the plane in the channel and cut the flute. Make as many passes as are necessary for the plane to cut the flute's entire width, from line to line.

When flutes are closed (do not run from end

Illus. 12-30. Lay out fillet flutes by using a ratio of 2-1. Each flute is twice as wide as the fillet. In this case, by using a 24-hole index head you will make each flute two holes wide and each fillet one hole wide.

to end, or terminate at some other detail), a plane cannot be used. They have to be completely carved by hand with a carving gouge that is about the same width as the flutes. To help you begin and end all the flutes at the same height on the turning, make light layout lines with a pencil.

Flutes usually have a round end. The carving gouge makes this end nicely as it begins the cut. Be sure the cut starts at the layout line and maintains an even depth along the length of the flute. Also, prevent the gouge from wandering outside the flute's layout lines. (See Illus. 12-32.)

The other end of the flute will also terminate with a round end, which is difficult to make when completing a cut. As the carving tool exits and rises out of the flute it is cutting

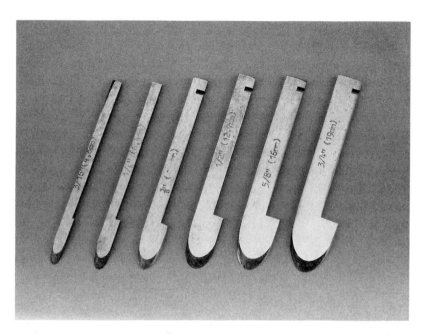

Illus. 12-31. A set of round cutters for a Stanley #45. They will make flutes that vary in size. (Tools courtesy of Woodcraft Supply)

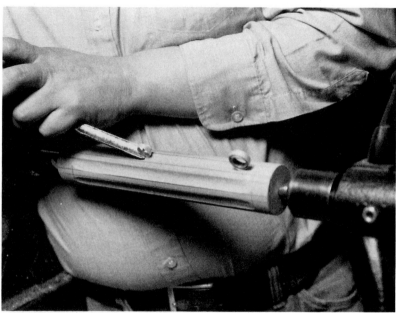

Illus. 12-32. Carving flutes with a gouge is not difficult, although it does require some care and attention.

against the grain. To solve this problem, cut almost the entire length of the flute in one direction. Stop just short of the other end and start a second cut in the opposite direction. (Be sure to begin at the second layout line.) When the two cuts meet, you simply have to blend them together. (See Illus. 12-33.)

If you want your flutes to end abruptly, you once again need to make fine pencil lines that mark the beginning and end. Cut the ends of the flutes with the pointed tip of a utility knife or a hobby knife. The gouge should be able to trim cleanly up to these knife cuts. (See Illus. 12-34.)

Making Stop Flutes

Stop flutes are laid out the same way as reeds. In fact, their bottom ends are reeds, while on the upper end of the turning are arris flutes, the type used in the Doric order.

Make a light scribe line where the reeds end. Carve the flutes using the techniques described above. Start as close to the reeds as possible. Next, carve the reeds as described above. The reeds have a rounded end where they turn into flutes. Make this end with a plunge cut from a

Illus. 12-33. The gouge cannot complete a round-ended flute, because rising out of the cut it would run against the grain. Start back from the other end of the flute and meet the first cut.

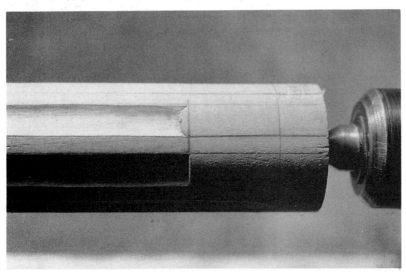

Illus. 12-34. Flutes can terminate in two other ways. The first way is a straight and abrupt end. Cut this end with a sharp utility knife. The second end is concave and is done by making a plunge cut with a carving gouge, as shown here. The gouge will easily clean up the narrow corners of the termination.

carving gouge, as described above. (See Illus. 12-35.)

Using a carving chisel, clean up the transition between the reed and the flute. A utility or a hobby knife might be necessary, to reach into the corners.

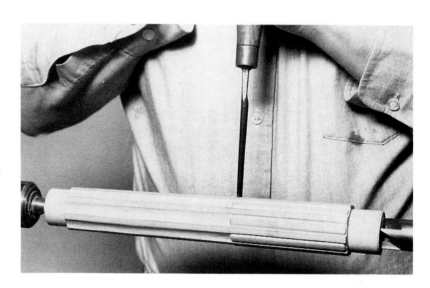

Illus. 12-35. The flutes and reeds in stop fluting are carved the same way as regular flutes and reeds. The ends of the reeds are also rounded with plunge cuts made with a carving gouge.

13
SPIRAL TURNINGS

At various times over the past several centuries, a form of decoration that is called either spiral or twist turnings has come into and gone out of fashion. During the late 1600s, this decoration was popular on William and Mary furniture. Later it became almost synonymous with the Empire period (1815–1840). (See Illus. 13-1.) During the Georgian period (1750–1800),

Illus. 13-1. Rope or spiral turnings are very closely associated with the Empire period. In this case, they are being used on a drop leaf table leg.

spiral-turned stair balusters were common in finer houses and on the "flame" finials on case furniture. Although there are numerous varieties of spiral turnings, they are all made basically the same way.

A spiral turning resembles a barber pole made of wood. Like reeds and flutes, the details are really carved, not turned. However, the spirals are always carved on a turning.

There are two basic types of spiral turnings. The first is a convex spiral turning. In a convex spiral turning, a number of different "strands" spiral together up the surface of the turning, creating an effect that looks very much like rope. In fact, this first type of spiral is also sometimes called "rope turning." This is the version so closely identified with Empire furniture. (See Illus. 13-1.) During that period, these rope-like decorations were used on the engaged columns on the fronts of chests, secretaries, and sideboards. They were used on table legs, bedposts, chair crests, and were even split (sawn in half) to make mirror pilasters.

The second type of spiral turning is concave. There are two versions of this type. The first is the same as the rope turnings described above in that there are several strands. However, each strand is concave, rather than convex. This type of spiral turning was occasionally used by the Romans on architectural columns in place of flutes. For this reason, they are called spiral flutes.

Spiral flutes were common on the finials of high-style Chippendale-period case furniture. The effect is suggestive of a candle flame, and for that reason these spiral-fluted finials are often called flame finials.

The second type of concave spiral turning is

colloquially referred to as "barley twist" or "barley sugar" turnings. These turnings are usually seen on William and Mary furniture, often used on legs or on stiles in the backs of chairs. This type of concave spiral turning has but two strands, so that when carved it looks like a piece of twisted pastry dough or a wet towel that you have twisted to wring the water out of it.

Although spiral turnings are closely associated with different furniture periods, you can still use them even if, rather than reproducing, you design your own work.

Carving Spiral Turnings

When laying out and carving spiral turnings, it may be helpful to compare them to the threads of a screw. The threads of a screw have both pitch and lead. Pitch refers to the number of threads per inch. It is a count of the number of times a ridge and adjacent groove occur on a single inch of the shank. Lead is the distance the thread travels along the shank in a single spiral.

While a screw has only a single worm that spirals up its shank, spiral turnings have several or more strands that spiral perfectly parallel to each other. What most interests the woodworker when making spiral turnings is the number of strands and their individual thickness.

Begin with a turning blank. If the turning has no squares, you can use a riven blank. This is sometimes helpful, as riven wood has a uniform grain and is, therefore, easier to carve. If it is necessary that the turning have a square section, such as on a table leg, you will have to start with a turning square.

When selecting the species of wood for a spiral turning, remember that you have to perform two separate operations. You have to turn the blank round, and then carve the actual spirals. The properties that make wood turn well do not necessarily make it carve well. For example, rock maple turns cleanly and crisply, but it is difficult to carve. Pine carves well, but it does not turn cleanly. Moderately hard woods like mahogany and walnut are often good compromises.

Carving Procedures

As with reeds, spirals can be carved into the surfaces of many turned elements. They are found on cylinders, tapers, bobbins, balls, vases, and urns. No matter what shape you are using, the process is the same. First, turn the blank to shape.

The next step is to divide horizontally the area to be spiralled. Before beginning, disconnect the plug on the lathe motor to avoid the chance of an accidental startup. Then determine how many separate strands will make up the spiral turning. The area will then be divided into that many equal horizontal segments.

You can determine the individual strands in two ways. You can use the index head as described in Chapter 12, or you can walk the segments off with a pair of dividers. It is easiest if you do this on the location line that corresponds to the part's greatest diameter. On a vase, this point would be the thickest part of the body.

Next, lay the center locator on the lathe bed. (See Chapter 12.) Push the pencil against the turning and trace a line the length of the section to be spiral-carved. (See Illus. 13-2.) Rotate the turning until the next point (determined by the index head or the dividers) aligns with the center locator, and trace a second horizontal line. Repeat this process as many times as you have strands.

Next, use a pair of dividers to divide the area that will be carved into equal vertical sections. How many sections you have will regulate the lead. The closer these lines are together, the shorter the lead. The farther apart they are, the longer it will be.

Make a pencil mark at each point where the leg of the dividers makes contact. Next, turn on the lathe and touch a soft lead pencil to each of the marks. This will result in a series of parallel vertical lines (called lead lines) around the diameter that intersect at right angles with the horizontal lines. Do not scribe these lead lines, as the scratches will remain in the finished spirals.

The result should be a uniform grid. The segments of the grid are not necessarily squares, but will be referred to as squares. Next, begin at one of the left-end squares and sketch a line from the bottom left-hand corner to the opposite upper corner. Continue the line from the abutting lower corner of the next square to the opposite upper corner. Repeat this process. You will have to slowly revolve the turning as you sketch a single spiralling line. (See Illus. 13-4.) At this point (while there is still only one line) you can best appreciate and understand the concept of lead. On the spiral turning I am making in Illus. 13-2–13-5, a single twist travels 6¼ inches.

When this spiral line (connecting the corners of the squares and connecting squares that are catercornered to each other) reaches the end of the turning, return to the beginning and start the sketching process anew. This time, start in the lower corner of the next square, above or below the one where the last spiral began. Repeat the process until there are as many lines as there are strands, spiralling from one end to the other. (See Illus. 13-5.)

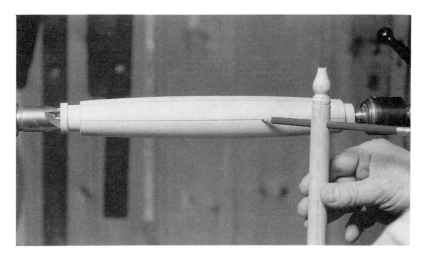

Illus. 13-2. Begin by using the center locator to divide the turning into as many horizontal segments as you will have strands. In this case, there are six segments.

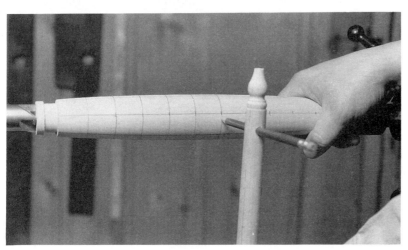

Illus. 13-3. Walk off the vertical lead lines with a pair of dividers. Here eleven vertical lines have been used. You can make the lead lines by turning on the lathe and touching a pencil to each mark. You can also hold the center locator in place and revolve the turning by hand, as shown here.

Illus. 13-4. The last two steps resulted in a grid over the entire area to be carved. Make a pencil line that connects the opposing corners of each square. If you start at the lower left corner of the left-hand (headstock) end, you will create a left-hand lead. Start at the upper left corner right end for a right-hand lead. The line you make will eventually spiral the length of the turning. The lead (the distance required to make one revolution) for the spiral shown here is 6¼ inches.

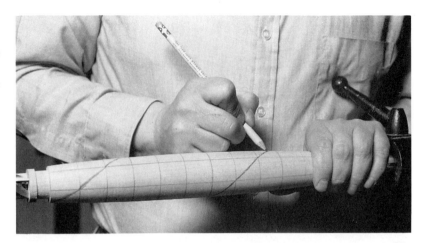

Illus. 13-5. Next, repeat the same process for all the other strands.

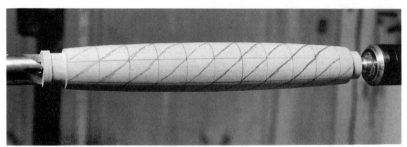

Note that on the turning in Illus. 13-2–13-5, the strands have a left-hand spiral, the opposite of an ordinary screw which has a right-hand thread. You can make strands with right-hand spirals if you want. In that case, you would begin at the upper left-hand corner of the first square and sketch a line that connects to the lower right-hand corner. Complete the grid as explained above, only going in the opposite direction.

The American Empire mirror shown in Illus. 13-6 illustrates the effects right- and left-hand spirals can create. Note that the pilasters have different-hand spirals, so they draw the viewer's eye into the mirror, instead of off to one side, as two spirals of the same hand would do.

You are now ready to begin the carving. As with reeding and fluting, it is easiest to carve while the turning is still held in the lathe. The lathe is serving as a carver's vise. Move the lathe

Illus. 13-6 (right). The left pilaster on this Empire-period mirror has a left-hand lead. The right pilaster has a right-hand lead.

away from the wall, so you can have access from in front of it and behind it. If possible, lock your indexing head, as this will help keep the turning from rotating while it is being carved.

Start at the beginning of one of the sketched spiral lines and with a ¼-inch carver's parting tool, cut a V groove along the line. Follow the spiral from corner to corner of each of the squares, trying to keep the cut at a constant depth. Return to the beginning and do the same to the adjacent spiral. (See Illus. 13-7.) Complete all the spiralled lines in the same manner.

Next, round the individual strands with a carving chisel. A ¾-inch chisel does the job nicely. You will be able to cut in only one direction without running against the grain. You can shape the lower half of each spiral by moving left to right in the same direction as you sketched the line. In order to round the upper half, you will have to stand on the other side of the lathe so as to be cutting with the grain. Because you have changed positions, you will

still be working left to right even though the direction of motion is now from headstock to tail stock. (See Illus. 13-8.)

After rounding with the chisel, smooth away the faceted tool cuts with a file. (See Illus. 13-9.) Use a half round file, because its curved side meets the flat side at a sharp edge. This edge is important for cleaning up between two spirals and creating a smooth flowing line. (A square edge would cut into the sides of the spiral that is adjacent to the one that is being smoothed.) File in two directions, so as to avoid filing against the grain. The surface left by the file is uniformly round, but needs to be smoothed further with sandpaper.

Spiral turnings are very adaptable, and you can create lots of different effects with them. Lead can be increased by placing the vertical lead lines farther apart, and can be decreased in the opposite manner. This has the effect of stretching out the spirals or compressing them. Also, you can vary the width of the strands including either more or less of them.

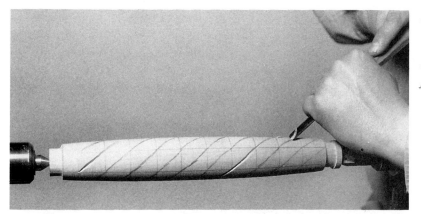

Illus. 13-7. Begin to carve the spirals by scoring the spiralling lines with a carver's V parting tool. Do all six lines. Try to achieve a uniform depth of cut.

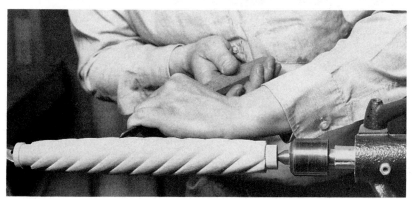

Illus. 13-8. Round the edges of the V grooves with a flat carving chisel. Because of the grain direction, you will sometimes have to stand in front of the lathe, and sometimes behind it.

Illus. 13-9. Finish rounding the spirals with a file, and sand carefully.

Carving Spiral Flutes

Spiral flutes are laid out the same way as are the rope turnings described above. Their lead is regulated by the number and spacing of the vertical lines, while the number of concave strands is determined by the number of horizontal segments. They can also be made with right- and left-hand spirals.

The strands on spiral flutes are concave, like the straight flutes described in Chapter 12. They are arris flutes, in that there is no fillet separating the flutes. So, you carve the spiral flute with a carving gouge, following the flute around the turning, as is done when carving concave rope turnings. (See Illus. 13-10.) Smooth each spiral flute with a piece of sandpaper wrapped around a round object of the proper diameter, such as dowel. (See Illus. 13-11.)

Illus. 13-10. Spiral flutes are laid out the same as twist turnings. However, the flutes are carved with a gouge.

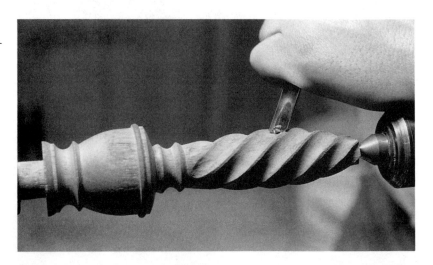

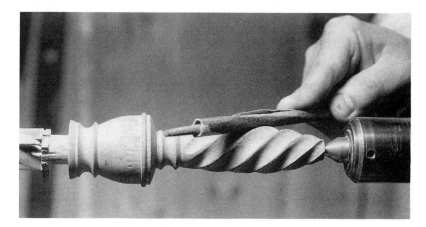

Illus. 13-11. Spiral flutes are easily cleaned up with sandpaper wrapped around something round, in this case a round file.

Barley Twists

Barley twist turnings are different from spiral flutes in that there are only two strands: one concave (the ridge) and the other convex (the groove). There are two varieties of barley twist. The first looks very much like twisted pastry dough. Each twist of the ridge (one complete twist equals the lead) butts directly against the twists above and below it. The groove is a shallow V shape, as can be found on rope turnings. This type of barley twist was commonly used on Federal period mirrors.

On the second type of barley twist, the groove is a deep concave U shape that distinctly defines each twist of the ridge. In fact, this version is very dramatic, for it appears to be hollow, as if a length of pastry dough had been wrapped around a narrow tube and the tube withdrawn.

Both types of barley twists generally begin with a cylinder, and are laid out the same way. First, use a skew to plane the cylinder so that it is perfectly smooth. Using the center locator, begin by dividing the cylinder into four equal horizontal segments. Next, set a pair of calipers to the cylinder's diameter and transfer that diameter to a pair of dividers. Walk off the diameter along one of the horizontal lines. Turn on the lathe and, with a #2 pencil, make the points into vertical lead lines. (See Illus. 13-13.) Make these lead lines very heavy, as they have to stand out. The result so far is a grid of fairly large squares.

Illus. 13-12. Both this Flemish fauteuil (left) and the Cromwellian chair make heavy use of barley twists. Note the use of right- and left-hand leads on the horizontal stretchers. Both right-arm stumps have a left-hand lead, while the left stumps have right-hand lead.

Illus. 13-13. To make barley twists, begin with a cylinder. Divide it into four horizontal segments with the center locator. Measure the diameter with a pair of calipers and transfer that measurement to a pair of dividers. Walk off the vertical lead lines and complete them around the turning, as shown here. Note that Illus. 13-13—13-21 were taken from behind the lathe and do not show the work as you, the turner, would see it.

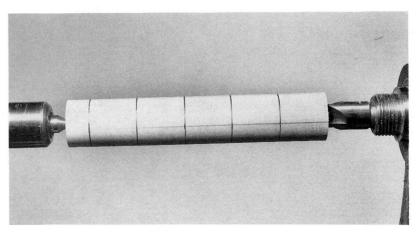

Set the dividers to ¼ the diameter of the cylinder, and walk that length off on one of the horizontal lines, vertically dividing each square into quarters. Turn on the lathe and complete these quarter lines, only make them noticeably lighter than the lead lines. (See Illus. 13-14.) The end result of all this layout work is a grid of four horizontal segments and a series of heavy vertical lead lines, with the space between divided into fourths by lighter "quarter" lines.

The heavy lead lines mark the length of each complete twist. In other words, the spiral's lead is equal to the cylinder's diameter. The quarter lines are necessary because it would be difficult to draw a perfect spiral that connected the corners of the large squares (horizontal segments and lead lines). Using the quarter lines, you have better control over the spiral, as the distance from corner-to-corner is so much shorter.

Still, these squares are long enough that an additional guide is helpful. Use a small piece of stiff paper, and lay it so that its edge connects the corners. Trace the spiral by running the pencil point along the paper's edge. (See Illus. 13-15.) Move the paper as necessary. The end result should be a perfect spiral. Choose any of the four horizontal lines, and the twist should meet at the intersection of that line and each of the lead lines.

In Illus. 13-15—13-21, I am making a left-hand spiral. However, a right-hand spiral can be easily made.

Illus. 13-14. Divide the distance between the heavy lead lines into quarters. Make the quarter lines lighter, so as not to confuse yourself.

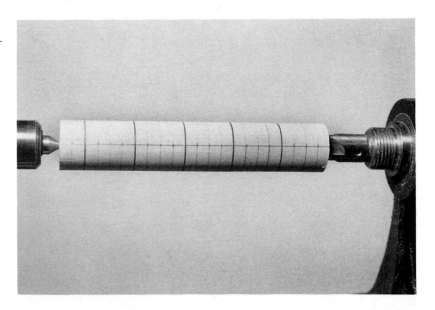

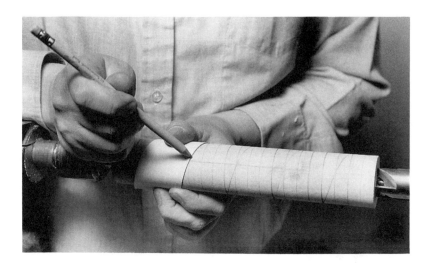

Illus. 13-15. Using a piece of flexible cardboard with a straight edge, connect the opposing corners of the quarter squares. To make a left-hand lead, start at the headstock end. Begin at the tail stock end to make a right-hand lead. Note that the spiral's lead corresponds to the lead lines. In other words, the width between lead lines is the distance travelled in one revolution.

As a point of interest for reproducers, barley twists were most popular during the 17th century, when they were used on chair and table legs. These pieces typically had an H stretcher. All three members (the two sides and the medial stretcher) usually had barley twists as well. Each member had a square in the center that separated a short right- and a left-hand spiral.

In Chapter 8, it was noted that horizontal members are usually symmetrical, so they divide in the center into mirror images. By making one a left-hand barley twist and another a right-hand barley twist, both ends of the stretcher are mirror images of each other. The next step in making the barley twist is to adhere a strip of masking tape to the blade of a small backsaw (about 10 inches long). If you are making the first type of barley twist, the distance between the points of the teeth and the tape should be about ⅛ the cylinder's diameter. For the hollow second type of twist, the distance should be about ¼ the diameter. In laying out the quarter lines, you already set a pair of dividers to this measurement. Use them. With the spiral line as a guide, cut a continuous spiral kerf that is as deep as the masking tape. (See Illus. 13-16.)

With a carving gouge (I use a #7 sweep, 25 mm wide), rough-out the groove by making downward cuts on each side of the kerf. (See Illus. 13-17.) Cut to the bottom of the saw kerf to make sure that it is eliminated from the

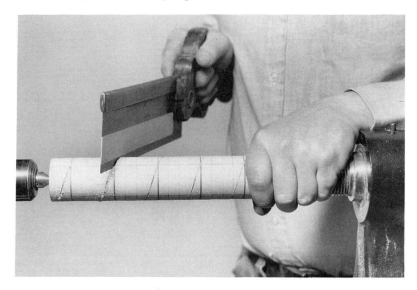

Illus. 13-16. Masking tape on the blade of a backsaw will help you control the depth of the saw kerf.

Illus. 13-17. Rough-out the spiral by making plunge cuts with a carving chisel. The chisel shown here is 35mm, and has a #3 sweep. Drive the gouge with a mallet. This is fast, rough work.

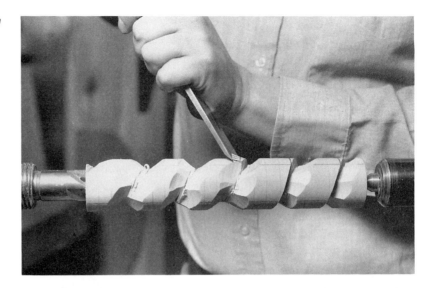

Illus. 13-18. Rough-round the spiral by turning the gouge over and using it upside down.

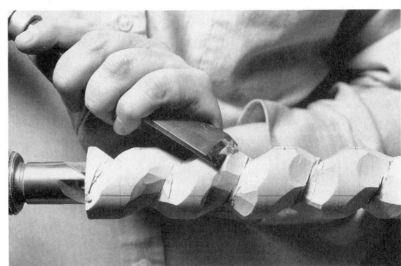

Illus. 13-19. Round the first type of barley twist with a square-cornered sanding block.

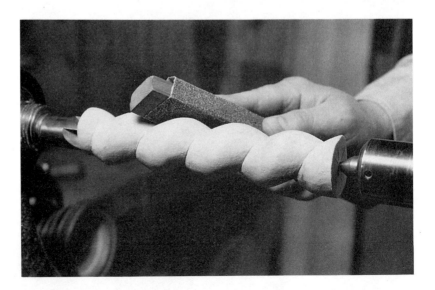

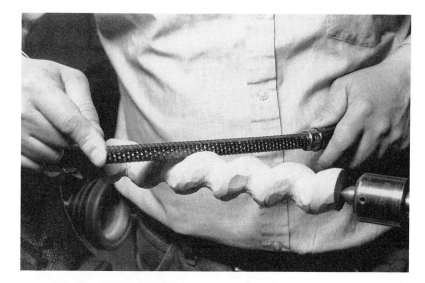

Illus. 13-20. If you are making hollow barley twists, shape the concave spiral with a round Surform.®

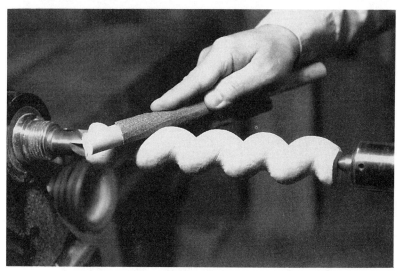

Illus. 13-21. Sand the twist with a piece of sandpaper wrapped around a dowel of the appropriate diameter.

completed twist. Do this along the entire spiral. Next, round the ridges with a wide, shallow carving gouge (I use #3 sweep, 35 mm), held upside down (bezel up). (See Illus. 13-18.)

If you are making the first type of barley twist, you are almost finished. Do as much smoothing as possible with the gouge. Then round the twist with a square-cornered sanding block. (See Illus. 13-19.)

If you are making the hollow type of barley twist, use a round rasp or a round Surform® to make a deep U-shaped groove between the ridges. (See Illus. 13-20.) Be sure to keep the groove an equal depth all along the turning. When the twist is fully formed, smooth the rasp marks with a piece of sandpaper wrapped around a dowel. You will also have to do some sanding to smooth the ridges. (See Illus. 13-21.)

14

CHAIR STILES

Woodworkers who have made chairs know how important it is to have the chair back extend beyond the rear edge of the seat. This configuration allows the sitter to recline slightly, and makes sitting in the chair more comfortable. Of course, this position also creates problems in that it moves the sitter's center of gravity back beyond the edge of the seat, putting him at risk of falling over backwards.

To prevent the chair from tipping over, it is equally important that the rear legs also extend beyond the back edge of the seat. (See Illus. 14-1.) This moves the chair's pivot point back behind the sitter's center of gravity, making it unlikely that the chair could fall over. The sitter would have to consciously tilt it on its pivot point by rocking it backwards on its rear legs.

On most chairs, the parts that make the sitter comfortable (while at the same time protecting him from an accidental backwards fall) are the two uprights whose lower ends form the rear legs, and whose upper ends form the stiles. In this regard, cabinetmakers have always had an advantage over the craftsmen who made turned chairs (chairs whose major parts are made in the lathe). Cabinetmakers can saw these parts out of solid 2-inch-thick plank in a shape that extends the stiles and back legs beyond the edge of the seat. The stiles can be then decorated with either carving or mouldings. Some stiles are left plain.

Chairmakers who made turned chairs did have some options that allowed them to create a reclining back while placing the pivot point beyond the seat's rear edge. Fancy chairmakers bent the leg/stile. (See Illus. 14-2.) On a Windsor chair, the back and rear legs are separate

Illus. 14-1. When you view a cabinetmaker's chair from the side, you can see how the leg/stile is shaped to accommodate the sitter, while preventing the chair from tipping over rearwards.

Illus. 14-2. Fancy chairmakers steam-bent the leg/stile.

Illus. 14-3. On a Windsor chair, the stile and leg are two separate parts, and can be angled for both comfort and safety.

systems anchored into the solid wooden seat. (See Illus. 14-3.) They can be angled as the chairmaker desires.

However, ladder-back-type chairs (banister backs, fiddlebacks, etc.) with turned legs/stiles pose some problems. How do you turn an elaborate stile and still make the chair comfortable and safe? The part has to be straight in order to be turned, and you cannot bend it later without the wood shearing where the turned decorations cut through layers of grain. (It is only possible for Fancy chairmakers to do this because their leg/stiles are completely unadorned.) Unable to easily and economically overcome these problems, many turned chairmakers simply used straight leg/stiles. The results were an uncomfortable chair that tipped over easily. (See Illus. 14-4.)

Around the turn of the 17th century and extending to the mid-18th century (late 1600s and mid-1700s), turned chairmakers often used another technique to create the desired leg/stile shape. They used this method to make Flemish chairs (caned-back chairs of the William and Mary period) as well as banister backs. (See Illus. 14-5 and 14-6.) The technique was revived by some Philadelphia cabinetmakers working in the Sheraton style (c. 1800), and was again used in the early 20th century during the Colonial Revival period. It was also favored by Edward G. Hyder. It is a handy technique for reproduction woodworkers, but can also be adapted by today's craftsmen/designers.

The leg/stile blank is sawn out of solid wood in the same manner used by cabinetmakers, but, like any part that is spindle-turned, it has to have two centers. The first center is located

Illus. 14-4 (left). As nice as the turnings are on this banister-back chair, its straight back makes it uncomfortable to sit on, and its straight, rear legs make it easy to tip over. Illus. 14-5 (right). This banister back is an improvement over the one shown in Illus. 14-4. The back reclines, but the rear legs (and the pivot point) are still directly below the sitter.

Illus. 14-6. This turned Flemish chair is both comfortable and well-balanced. Its stiles recline for comfort, while the second bend places the pivot point behind the sitter's center of gravity.

on the upper end of the stile. However, because the part has two angles in it, the lathe's other center cannot be aligned with the other end of the blank. (See Illus. 14-7.) You have to turn the part using an artificial center located on a box-like bracket that you have to make. This is a simple project, and it should pose no problems. While the stile is being turned, the leg end of the blank is held in this bracket. (See Illus. 14-8 and 14-9.)

This bracket is essentially two sheets of ¼-inch-thick plywood with two specially shaped shim blocks inside. The space between the blocks is the same as the outline of the rear leg. When the blank is placed in this space and the bracket reassembled, the part is held securely. The box also has a bottom board in which the second center is located.

Note that when assembled the box and the projecting stile section of the blank look very much like a Russian balalaika, a banjo-type instrument with a triangular body. (See Illus. 14-10.) This triangular shape is important, for its weight is evenly distributed, even though the leg/stile blank is an irregular shape. As a result of this even distribution of weight, the

box and blank spin as one unit with little vibration. Of course, you should still turn at a slow speed, at approximately 600 RPM. (See Illus. 14-11.)

The following distinctions are a point of historical interest for those who make reproductions. On banister backs, usually just the stile was turned. However, on Flemish chairs, both the stile and rear leg were more commonly turned. This means that to reproduce most Flemish chairs, you have to make two such brackets—one for turning the stile and the other for turning the rear leg.

Turning the rear leg is quite easy, for it is no more than two cylinders placed between round-ended squares. These squares are strategically located to accommodate the joints for the side and rear stretchers and seat rails. In practice, the leg end of a Flemish-type leg/stile is turned first, for the squares will still allow the part to be held securely in the bracket. The stile end is turned second.

Since you will have to assemble and disassemble the box every time you turn a leg/stile, I suggest holding it together with carriage bolts rather than screws. Glue the interior forms to

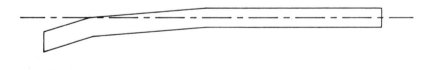

Illus. 14-7. The shape of a leg/stile blank will prevent it from being placed between a lathe's two centers.

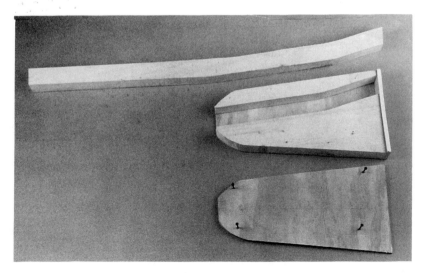

Illus. 14-8. To turn a sawn leg, you need to provide a second center. This is done with a box-like bracket that is made in the shop.

Illus. 14-9. An exploded view of the bracket you need to make to turn leg/stiles.

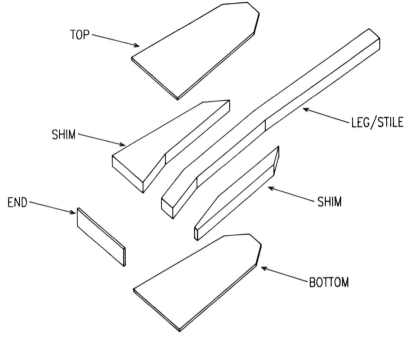

Illus. 14-10. When the part is in the box, the assembly looks like a Russian balalaika.

Illus. 14-11. To minimize vibration, turn chair/stiles at about 600 RPM.

one of the sheets of plywood so that they do not move when you are mounting or dismounting a part. Screw the rear board in place. Due to slight variations that occur in the shape of handmade leg/stile blanks, the center and spurs (I mount the bracket on the drive center) are not always located on exactly the same spot. Moving the center around will eventually chew a depression in the rear board, but, because of the screws, it can be easily replaced.

Also note that the bracket's corners (closest to the stile) are rounded. This protects your left wrist and elbow. If the corners remain square, they could give you a nasty whack. Indeed, while turning leg/stiles, be very conscious of the fact that the wide end of the assembly is essentially two spinning wings. Shut off the lathe if you need to walk by it.

Even though the bracket is a simple project, it still requires time and effort to make. Such a bracket is also limiting, in that each one you make fits a blank of one precise shape. You do have the options of varying the design of the turning that you make using the box or varying the straight stile's length (as long as you do not exceed your lathe's capacity). However, you cannot change the leg/stile's overall shape. Therefore, you are more likely to use this technique when you are making a production run of a particular chair design, or if you are going to add that chair to your product line and will be making small quantities frequently.

If you plan on making just one chair, there is a simplified technique you can use, but it is more wasteful of wood. In this case, first cut the leg/stile blank to the same shape as the entire assembly shown in Illus. 14-10, although overall the triangular area will be slightly smaller than the bracket's outside dimensions. Turn the stile, and then saw the waste off the leg. (See Illus. 14-12.) As noted, this is very wasteful, especially in contrast to using the

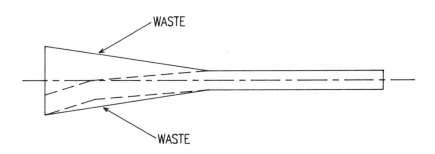

Illus. 14-12. You can make leg stiles this way, and cut away the extra material after the stile has been turned. However, this is very wasteful, and is only practical if you are making just one chair.

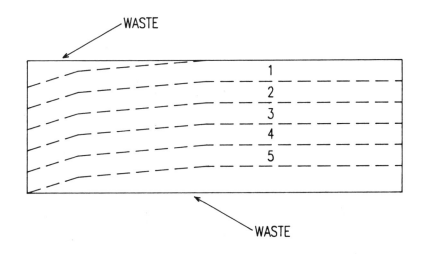

Illus. 14-13. The most economical way to make leg stiles is to nest them.

bracket, as in that case leg/stiles blanks are "nested" and cut out one from inside the other. (See Illus. 14-13.)

There is yet another method that is a modification of this technique and is slightly less wasteful. Saw the stile and one half of the balalaika shape out of solid plank. A blank of this shape is badly out of balance, so you will have to add a counterweight to prevent it from vibrating with enough force to make your lathe "walk" across the shop floor. Therefore, attach a wedge with dry wall screws (that are strategically placed so that they bore into the leg) where the stretcher and seat rail mortises will be cut. (See Illus. 14-14.) This way, the screw holes will not remain in the finished part. However, you still have to cut a sizable amount of

waste from the leg because they cannot be "nested."

A woodworker friend of mine once used a modification of the process just described. Instead of a wedge, he made a bracket that could be slipped over the blank. The bracket had a cast-iron counterweight that could be adjusted along a metal rod. The weight was moved along the rod to a spot that exactly counterbalanced the blank, and was then held in place with a setscrew. However, one day the setscrew slipped while the lathe was turning, and the two pound counterweight was hurled across the shop as if it were shot from a cannon. Luckily no one was hurt. This experiment, obviously, proved to be unsuccessful.

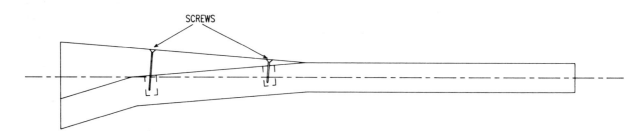

Illus. 14-14. Here is another technique you can try if you are making only a few chairs. Attach a wedge-shaped piece of wood to the blank with dry wall screws.

Make sure that you bore them into the location of the seat and stretcher mortise, so that their holes do not remain in the finished part.

15

TURNING DISCS

Most of the furniture and building parts made in a lathe are turned between centers. Remember, this type of work is also called spindle-turning. The term accurately describes such parts as legs and balusters, which are spindles. However, occasionally you have to make a project that requires you to turn disc-shaped parts. Included in this chapter are two examples. The first is the top of a stool. The second is the top of a candle stand. These two pieces have been selected because each uses one of the two processes for turning disc-shaped parts. (Chapter 16 also explores ways to turn some disc-shaped architectural parts.)

Before attempting these processes be forewarned: Your lathe may not have the capacity to be used for either process. The lathe requirements are described below.

The stool top is turned between centers, just as are the legs and stretchers. However the blank is very different in shape from those used in spindle-turning. Instead of using a long and slender turning square ripped from the edge of a plank, begin with a slab of wood cut from the end of a piece of lumber. The blank used for the stool top began as a piece of 2-inch-thick plank, 14 inches square.

Because you are turning a part for a piece of furniture, the species of wood used may depend on the species you are using for the rest of the project. For example, if the other parts are mahogany, which you want to cover with a natural finish, you will probably want to make the top of mahogany as well. However, in the event you are planning to paint the project, you only have to be concerned with the wood's working properties.

Normally, Windsor chair seats are made of pine or some other soft wood. However, pine is too soft to turn cleanly. I instead use walnut for the top.

The size of the plank you begin with is, of course, dependent on the job, but is also determined by your lathe's capacity (see Chapter 1), specifically, its swing—twice the distance between the lathe's centers and the bed. Its swing is the maximum diameter you can turn. In other words, a lathe that measures 6 inches from center to bed has a 12-inch swing. You could not turn a 14-inch stool top on a lathe with that capacity.

On many lathes, the amount of swing available for turning disc-shaped parts is greatly increased by a gap in the bed, located just under the drive center. This gap will increase the swing by several inches. Another way to increase the swing is to block up (or elevate) the head and tail stock, as was done to the lathe shown in Illus. 15-1.

Before chucking up the blank for the stool top, take a pair of dividers and trace a circle that is slightly larger than the finished diameter (but not greater than the lathe's swing). (See Illus. 15-2.) Cut out the circle using a band saw or a bow saw. If you do not have either one, cut off the corners as close to the circumference as possible. (See Illus. 15-3.)

Chuck up the blank by pushing the drive center into the center mark made by the divider leg. If you like, remove the drive center and tap it in place with a mallet. Mount the blank and the center in the lathe, and push the tail stock into place. Tighten the tail center so that the blank is securely gripped on both sides. (See Illus. 15-4.)

Move the rest into position. You will have to

Illus. 15-1. The headstock, tail stock, and rest on this lathe have been blocked up to increase its swing. This makes it possible to turn discs up to 12 inches in diameter.

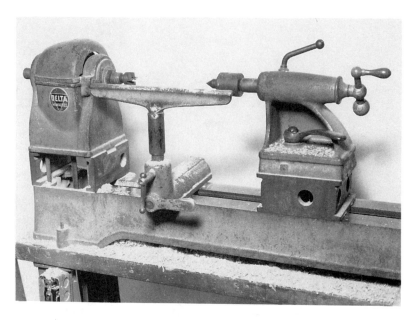

Illus. 15-2. Trace out the size disc you are going to turn with a pair of dividers, and saw out the circle.

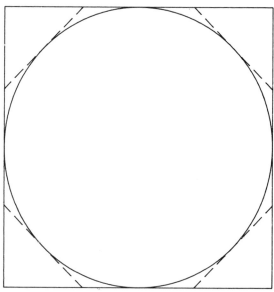

Illus. 15-3. If you don't have either a band saw or a bow saw, make your blank close to round by cutting off the corners like this.

slide the rest bracket close to the headstock and pull it towards you as far as it will come. It is possible that the rest will not pull out as far as the edge of the blank. This creates another constraint on the diameter size of the disc that you are turning. If you have this problem, try placing the rest so that it is catercornered against the bed. (See Illus. 15-5.) If you do this, you can add an inch or so on the maximum diameter of disc the rest will accommodate.

Set the lathe to the slowest possible speed. Remember, the farther the distance a point is from the center, the faster it is moving. Therefore, if your blank is 7 inches in radius (14 inches in diameter), its edge is spinning much faster than the lathe center and will strike against the tool with greater force than will a typical turning square. Also, the amount of vibration caused by the blank's eccentricity increases with the length of the radius.

Illus. 15-4. Place the drive center's point on the mark left by the stationary divider leg. Tighten the tail stock to grip the roughly rounded blank.

Illus. 15-5. Your rest's capacity may not be as great as the lathe's swing. If it isn't, you can add an extra inch or two by cocking the rest in relation to the bed.

Before turning on the lathe, spin the blank by hand to be sure that it will clear the rest and bed. Then, start the lathe and true the blank by trimming its outside edge. (See Illus. 15-6.) Instead of using a roughing gouge for this work, I use a ½-inch spindle gouge.

The blank will quickly become perfectly round and, as this happens, the vibration will decrease equally fast. Still, the disc will not turn smoothly, for while its outside edge is a perfect circle, the two surfaces are not spinning in a single plane.

To correct this, shut off the lathe and adjust the rest. You need to turn it 90 degrees to the bed, so place it across the disc's top face (the surface closest to the tail stock). On the finished part, this surface will be the top. Push the rest as close to the blank's top surface as possible, placing the end of the rest as close to the center as possible without having the two come

Illus. 15-6. Spin the rough blank by hand to make sure that it clears the rest. Then smooth the blank's outside edge.

into contact. (The rest only has to extend across half the blank's diameter in order for you to be able to cut the entire face).

Spin the blank to be sure that it clears the rest and that the rest clears the center. Turn on the lathe and, with a spindle gouge, joint the spinning surface. (See Illus. 15-7.) Begin on the outside edge, as this is the point on the radius where the disc is most eccentric. As you joint this surface, the disc will spin even more smoothly. Of course, you will not be able to joint the entire surface because the center is in

the way. If you shut off the lathe and examine the part, it is obvious that a protruding boss will remain when you take the stool top out of the lathe. It can be removed later.

To shape the other face (the top's lower surface), move the rest to the other side, the one closest to the head-stock. Once again the rest should be as close to the disc's surface as possible and its end must not be in contact with the center. Spin the disc by hand to be sure.

Joint the bottom surface as you did the upper. (See Illus. 15-8.) Any remaining vibration

Illus. 15-7. Move the rest and joint the tail-stock side of the blank—the side that will be the completed top's upper surface. Start jointing at the outer edge of the disc, as that is where it is most eccentric.

should now disappear. At this point, you have a perfect disc—its outside edge is a circle, and its two surfaces are perfectly parallel with each other. The lower surface too will have a boss that can be removed later.

However, the completed stool top is dished, not flat. Do this shaping next, also using a spindle gouge. The gouge will cut best if it is rolled on its side, the same way as is done when you are spindle-turning. (See Illus. 15-9.) Dish as deeply as you like. You may even have to readjust the rest if the distance between it and the disc's surface becomes too great. You will in-

crease the height of the boss projecting from the surface where the center makes contact.

You now have a stool top with a perfectly jointed bottom and a dished top. The next step is to contour the edge. Return the rest to its first position, and use a gouge to round the upper corner of the stool top. Remember, the back of the sitter's legs will be in contact with this edge. If it is left square and sharp, it might damage clothing or even cut off circulation. Blend the curved edge into the dished surface.

The stool top looks best if its lower edge is chamfered. The chamfering draws the edge's

Illus. 15-8. Move the rest and joint the headstock side.

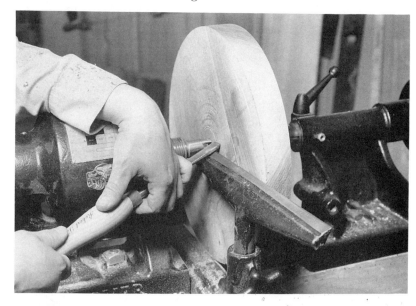

Illus. 15-9. Move the rest a third time and dish-out the top with a spindle gouge.

Illus. 15-10. Return the rest to the first position and contour the edge.

lower corner back out of the line of sight, eliminating the visual reference point that tells the viewer's eye how thick the top is. This technique makes the top appear much thinner, while in reality it is thick enough to create strong, long-lasting joints where the legs are attached. Do the chamfering with the gouge as well. (See Illus. 15-10.)

If you wish, you can also decorate the edge with some simple details such as one or two beads. These as made with a skew, but by scraping with the toe rather than a rolling cut with the heel.

Illus. 15-11. Grip the top between your workbench dogs and plane away drive center boss.

Take the stool top out of the lathe and secure it to the top of your workbench. One way is to use the tail vise and bench dogs to secure the stool top.

Remove the bottom protrusion first, as the top cannot sit flat on its bottom. It can be removed with a sharp bench plane. (See Illus. 15-11.) Turn the top on its now perfectly flat bottom and, with a fish-tail carving gouge, remove the boss. Sand the area smooth, so no evidence of it remains. (See Illus. 15-12.)

The candle-stand top is much thinner than the stool top, but can still be turned the same

way if your lathe has sufficient swing. However, another technique has been used for the one shown in this chapter. This process is known as faceplate turning. To use this process, you first have to own a faceplate.

A faceplate is a flat metal disc with several holes drilled through it. At the center is a raised hollow boss that is internally threaded with the same thread as is on the outside surface of the headstock spindle. (See Illus. 15-13.) This allows the faceplate to be mounted onto the spindle. (Before buying a faceplate, make sure that it will fit your lathe.) The boss also has hexagonal sides, so you can grip it with a wrench and tighten it onto the spindle. The threads are right hand, which means that the

faceplate screws onto the spindle in the direction opposite the lathe's rotation. Thus, the force of the wood against the cutting tool tightens the faceplate.

On many lathes, the headstock spindle is threaded on both ends. This means that one end is on the opposite side from the bed. If you need to turn a disc with a diameter greater than the lathe's swing, mount the faceplate on this end. This process is referred to as turning outboard.

To turn outboard, your lathe will need a special outboard rest. If it is not so equipped, you can have one fabricated (assuming the amount of outboard turning you need to do justifies the effort). Inboard turning is done on the end

Illus. 15-12. Invert the top and remove the tail-center boss with a fishtail carving gouge. Sand it smooth.

Illus. 15-13. A faceplate mounts on the headstock spindle and allows you to turn discs without using the tail stock.

of the spindle that overhangs the bed, using the regular rest.

Faceplates come in different diameters ranging from 3 to 6 inches. The narrow ones are used to turn small pieces, while the wider ones are for larger work. The faceplate is pierced by several countersunk holes, through which screws are passed to secure the work. Some faceplates have elongated slots rather than holes. These slots allow you to adjust the placement of the screws according to the size of the block of wood you are turning.

Of course, mounting a faceplate with screws means that there will be screw holes in the bottom of the completed part. This is not a problem on the top of a candle stand, as the top is secured to the pedestal with a cleat that completely hides the holes. Another way of dealing with screws is discussed below.

There is another problem when you use screws to mount a faceplate. The greater the piece's diameter, the more securely the screws need to be attached to the wood. This means that it is best to use longer screws with wider pieces. However, a piece like the candle stand top is very thin, and when you are dishing the top, your lathe tool may very well run into the screws. This will not only damage the tool, but when you extract the screws they will leave holes that completely pierce the top. This is not acceptable in a piece of furniture.

The way to prevent this from happening is to glue a shim block to the blank. The glue holds the blank to the shim, while the screws hold the shim to the faceplate. (See Illus. 15-14.) The shim can be as thick as the screws are long (or even thicker), thus eliminating the problems of holes that extend either all the way through the turned part or just into its bottom.

You can use just about any glue you want to fasten the shim to the blank. However, be sure to allow it to cure as long as the manufacturer recommends. You do not want the disc to fly off the faceplate because you were impatient. Bowl turners speed up the process by using "instant super" cyanoacrylate glue (sold under the brand name Hot Stuff) that dries immediately and creates a strong, sure bond. However, these glues are much more expensive than the white and yellow glues that can be bought at any hardware (or even grocery) store.

Before gluing the shim, joint the blank's rear surface, the one secured to the faceplate, with a jointer, thickness planer, or a hand plane. If you use a jointer or thickness planer, handplane the bottom anyway. This will remove the

Illus. 15-14. To avoid screw holes in the bottom of the finished part, glue a shim block to the blank and attach the faceplate to this shim.

chatter marks left by the machine. This surface will remain on the finished part (unless you have a problem with eccentricity, as discussed below), and such machine marks are inappropriate in fine woodworking, even on an unseen surface.

If you are gluing on a shim, make sure that its mating surface is also jointed. The two perfectly flat surfaces will create a dependable glue bond.

Make sure that the shim is centered on the blank. If it is not, the blank's outer edge will be very eccentric, and when rounding it, you will cut away some of its diameter. Also, the amount of eccentricity could exceed your lathe's capacity, making it impossible to turn the part at all without sawing away additional width.

The stand's top is turned in very much the same way as that for the stool. Begin by truing the blank's edge. If the blank and the shim each have parallel surfaces, the blank should be spinning smoothly in a single plane. If there is any eccentricity, joint the bottom (headstock) surface with a gouge.

If the bottom is eccentric, so is the top. Joint this surface as well before beginning the recessing and contouring. Rough out the recessed area with a gouge in basically the same way as was done with the stool top. However, there is one important difference: The top of the stool is dished. It is a long, concave curve. The top of the stand, although recessed from the rim, is otherwise flat. (See Illus. 15-15.)

Note that the rim is moulded, and like similar details on a spindle turning, is set off from the flat surface by a fillet. Use the point of a skew to lay out this fillet and to sever the wood fibres that run through it into the dished area. Using the skew's pointed nose, form the fillet. (See Illus. 15-16.)

A bowl turner would do the next step with a heavy tool with a square edge, called a straight scraper. However, since you are more likely to own a skew than a straight scraper, I will ex-

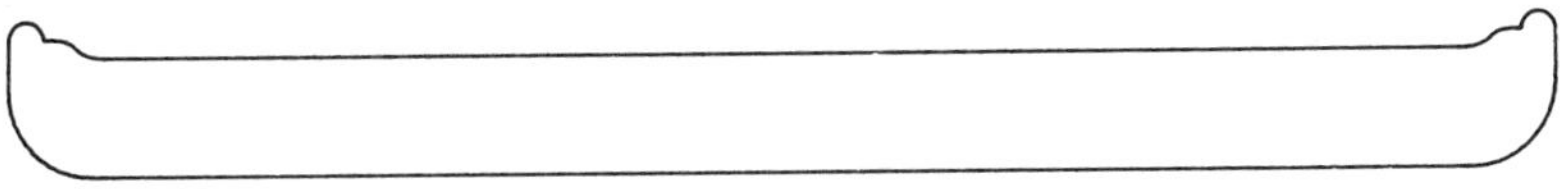

Illus. 15-15. The surface of the stool top is dished. It is a long, gentle curve. The top of the stand is recessed, but otherwise flat with a moulded rim.

Illus. 15-16. Form the rim fillet with a skew.

plain how to do the process using this tool.

Lay the skew on the flat side of its blade, rather than on the edge. Hold the cutting edge parallel to the surface of the spinning part, and raise its handle so that the tool is at a scraping angle. Using the skew as a scraper, use it to level and flatten the surface within the moulded edge. As you pass it back and forth, its straight edge will act in the same manner as the smooth plane you use to smooth boards on the bench. (See Illus. 15-17.) It will find and level any unevenness. Several passes may be necessary to trim all the high spots and eliminate any low spots.

Illus. 15-17. A skew will joint the dished-out area by eliminating any high spots.

Illus. 15-18–5-20. Examples of turned discs. The wheel on the spinning wheel shown here is a turned disc.

Illus. 15-19. Fireplace bellows.

Illus. 15-20. The shelves on a dumbwaiter.

As explained in Chapter 6, this sort of low-angle scraping causes a lot of heat and will quickly dull the cutting edge. However, this process is not something you will do often, and the skew's edge can be quickly restored by honing.

Finally, move the rest so that you can once again work on the part's underside. Using a gouge, contour the edge's lower corner. This step serves the same purpose as it did on the stool top. It pulls the corner back out of the line of sight so that it is no longer a visual reference point that indicates to the viewer precisely how thick the top is.

Both these processes for turning discs—the between-centers and faceplate techniques—can be used for many more purposes than just the two examples given in this chapter. The technique you choose to use for any of your projects is a function of your lathe's capacity, its fixtures, for example, whether the headstock spindle is threaded, and your preference. (See Illus. 15-18–15-20.)

16

KNOBS, PULLS, PEGS, AND OTHER PARTS

There are a number of other parts that both builders and furniture makers occasionally need to make that can be turned in a lathe. Some examples include wooden knobs for use on doors and lids, and pulls for drawers. Such wooden knobs have been used for centuries. While brass pulls have always been the most common for formal, high-style woodwork, wooden pulls are more usually associated with country woodwork. One exception is case fur-

Illus. 16-1. Mushroom-shaped drawer pulls are closely associated with the Empire period.

niture from the Empire period. This furniture generally had turned mahogany knobs. (See Illus. 16-1.) During this period, mahogany door knobs were sometimes used for passage (interior) doors. They were not used on exterior doors because mahogany cannot withstand the elements.

Only two general types of turned knob are possible. Both are usually known by colloquial names that refer to their shapes. They are the mushroom and the sausage knobs. Both names give you an indication of what these knobs look like.

The sausage knob is the earlier type of knob. It was used through much of the 18th century. (See Illus. 16-2.) As noted above, the mushroom knob became popular in the early 19th century, and was used on Empire furniture and as a passage door knob. The shape endured throughout the rest of that century and all of this one as well. Today, the mushroom knob is by far the more common shape, while sausage knobs are only seen on reproductions.

Both types of knobs have several features in common. The first feature is a narrow neck located behind a wider body. The neck provides a place for your fingers, while the body gives you something to grasp, either for pulling or turning. (See Illus. 16-3.)

Behind the neck is a flange, slightly smaller in diameter than the body. The flange's rear surface is flat and butts against the surface to which the knob is applied. Depending on their function, both mushroom and sausage knobs may have a stem—a narrow, round dowel projecting from the back of the flange. The stem is

Illus. 16-2. Sausage-shaped pulls were used during the 18th century.

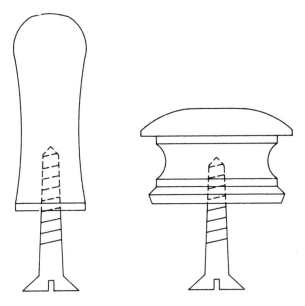

Illus. 16-3. Sausage knobs, shown at left, were used in the 17th and 18th centuries. Mushroom knobs, shown at right, became popular in the early 19th century, and have been made throughout the 20th.

almost always part of the turning, rather than a separate piece.

The stem fits through a hole. If the knob is glued into a hole, the stem acts as a tenon. A stem is also necessary on a lid or door because the knob often operates some form of catch, which keeps the door (or lid) closed. The knob shown in Illus. 16-4 has a stem with a tab attached to it. When the knob is turned, the tab engages a keeper or slides behind a jamb.

If a pull with a stem is used on a drawer, some form of cotter is necessary to prevent the stem from being pulled loose from the hole and to prevent it from turning. However, it is far more common for drawer pulls to be attached with a screw. The screw passes through a hole in the drawer front and is fastened into the back of the knob. Being larger than the hole, the screw's head prevents it from being pulled loose from the drawer. The screw's thread keeps the knob tight against the drawer front. Should the knob loosen, you can easily retighten it by turning it clockwise.

Most mushroom knobs have a smooth, slightly domed face. However, during the Victorian period some knobs were decorated with

Illus. 16-4. Some knobs keep doors closed. When they are used as such, they usually have some form of catch attached to their stems.

a series of rings on the front surface. The method for doing this is described on pages 180 and 182.

Another turned part similar to a knob and used in both building and furniture construction is the peg, a device on which other objects are hung. The widespread interest in Shaker woodworking has given them credit for the most popular peg design, which has been generically dubbed the "shaker peg." However, long before the Shakers arrived in America (1774), pegs were in common use. Even when the Shaker communities were at their peak, the world's peoples were making and using pegs that were indistinguishable from those used by the Shakers.

The most common use for pegs is hanging clothes, as, for example, hats and coats. However, both kitchen and bathroom towels are also hung this way. The Shakers even used pegs for hanging chairs off the floor and out of the way. (See Illus. 16-5.) Pegs are most often arranged in a row, being anchored into a wooden strip that is then screwed to the wall. However, some

hat and coat racks consist of a vertical post with a cluster of pegs.

Pegs are very much like knobs and pulls, except that they are usually longer and more narrow. They generally have a mushroom-shaped body with a very long neck. Since a peg is not pulled or twisted, its body should be long enough to hold whatever is hung from it. On the back end of the peg's neck there is generally a flange, and behind that a tenon (stem) that fits into a hole in the wooden strip. In other words, the tenon holds the peg securely in place so that the peg can hold something else.

Knobs and pegs are most efficiently made in pairs. They are attached by their fronts. To make a peg or knob, begin with a turning square about ¼ inch (the width of a parting tool) longer than twice the part's overall length. Round the square to the pull's maximum diameter, usually that of the body. Using the

Illus. 16-5. The Shakers used pegs to hang everyday items out of the way. They even hung their chairs from pegs. (Photo courtesy of Shaker Workshops, Concord, MA)

parting tool, make a shallow cut in the middle of the blank, at the point at which the knobs will be joined together. (See Illus. 16-6.) This cut will help you lay out the parts. Next, if the knobs have stems, make shallow cuts with the parting tool that lay out the flanges' rear surfaces.

Using a spindle gouge (¼ inch for the mushroom knob, perhaps ½ inch for the sausage knob), cut the neck. (See Illus. 16-7.) On a sausage-shaped knob, the neck is a shallow curve. On a mushroom pull, it is a deep cove.

The mushroom knob usually has a narrow fillet a short distance from the edge of the flange, and the flange appears more delicate if its rear corner is bevelled backwards slightly. This, too, can be done with a skew, although a diamond point is probably better for delicate work.

Separate the knobs with the parting tool. Leave them joined by a narrow section, perhaps ⅜ inch in diameter. (See Illus. 16-8.) Using a diamond point, make rolling cuts to round the front surfaces. Keep the flat side of the blade in continual contact with the wood. (See Illus. 16-9.) This will create a glassy smoothness.

Using the parting tool, completely separate

Illus. 16-6. Make a shallow parting cut to lay out a pair of knobs.

Illus. 16-7. Cut the knobs' necks with a lady finger gouge. These necks are basically deep coves.

Illus. 16-8. Separate the knobs by deepening the original parting cut.

Illus. 16-9. Face-off each knob with a diamond point, as there is not enough room in the groove for a skew.

the knobs while they are turning in the lathe. (See Chapter 5.) They will not fly loose. Instead, they simply fall onto the bed. You will then have two completed pulls with a small burr where they were parted. This can be removed with sandpaper. (See Illus. 16-10.)

In the exact center of each rear surface is a hole made by the lathe center (the drive center will also have the marks made by the spurs). Use this to locate the hole for the screw. Make this hole with a small twist drill that is narrower than the screw. This way, the screw will not split the knob, but its threads will still have a strong bite.

During the mid-19th century a more elaborate version of the mushroom pull became popular, and was used on Victorian period chests of drawers. The front surface of this knob was decorated with turned rings. The inspiration for these decorated mushroom knobs may well have been the stamped brass rosette drawer pulls associated with the late Sheraton style. (See Illus. 16-11.)

To make these knobs, you need either a small faceplate with a hole in its exact center or a screw chuck, which is even more effective. (See Illus. 16-12 and 16-13.) If you use the faceplate, attach the wooden blank with a single screw

Illus. 16-10. A burr will remain where the knobs are parted. Trim it off with a chisel and smooth the knobs with sandpaper.

Illus. 16-11. Decorated wooden knobs became popular during the mid-19th century, and may have been inspired by Sheraton-period brass rosette pulls.

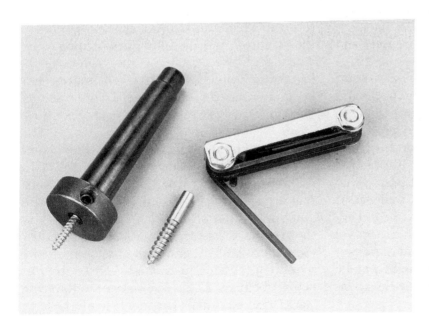

Illus. 16-12. To turn the surface of a drawer pull, you need a screw chuck. This one comes with two sizes of screws, which you can interchange by loosening the Allen screw. (Tools courtesy of Woodcraft Supply)

Illus. 16-13. A small faceplate with a screw hole in its center will also do the job. Always drill the pilot hole with a bit that is smaller than the screw.

through the center of the plate. That is all that holds the blank to the faceplate. The blank is so small, a single screw is all that is necessary to secure it.

Like a drive center, a screw chuck has a reverse-tapered self-locking shank that allows you to mount it in the headstock spindle. In its exact middle is a single screw on which the blank is mounted.

Begin with a short turning square the length of the knob and locate its center by marking an X on one end. Next, drill a pilot hole for the screw in the center of the blank. This pilot hole must be wide enough so that the screw does not split the blank, but narrow enough so that the threads bite securely into the wood. In fact, it is imperative that the threads hold securely and not strip inside the hole. The lathe turns against the direction of the threads, so the cutting action must not loosen the screw. Should the screw strip its hole, you will not be able to turn the blank because it will be prevented from spinning by the counterforce of the gouge.

You will not have to use the tail stock when using the screw chuck, so move it well out of the way, preferably to the far end of the bed. Place the tool rest close to the blank. If you are using a small faceplate, the disc may project beyond the blank and, so, you might not be able to get the rest as close to the work as normally preferred.

Round the blank and turn the knob to a mushroom shape. Cut the domed front surface with a skew, making a rolling cut, or, if you prefer, use a diamond point.

When the knob is complete, shut off the lathe and pivot the rest in its bracket so that it is at a right angle to the bed. Move the rest up as close to the front of the knob as is possible without the two rubbing. Now turn the ring decorations in the face. (See Illus. 16-14.)

Most of the tools you use in general spindle turning are probably too big to do fine, intricate decoration, although a ¼-inch gouge and skew will cut some simple shapes. If you have to make this type of pull frequently, or you want to do more of this delicate type of work, you should invest in some miniature turning tools. These tools are available through many catalogue tool suppliers. Except for their sizes, they are identical to the larger ones. They are sharpened and used the same way, as well. (See Illus. 16-15.)

Besides knobs, pulls, and pegs, other parts can also be turned with the screw chuck. Finials are the small, turned upright decorations that are often placed on top of case furniture and clocks. They usually sit on a plinth either at the corners of the pediment or in the center. (See Illus. 16-16.) Although they are usually more delicate and attenuated than knobs, finials can be turned on a screw chuck in the same way. However, finials are not usually held in

Illus. 16-14. Turning a decorated knob is very simple. Move the rest as close to the work as possible.

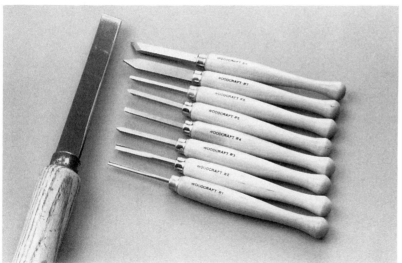

Illus. 16-15. A turning set of miniature tools is needed when you are turning some finials and pendants, or decorating the surface of mushroom pulls. These tools are identical to their larger counterparts, and are ground and sharpened the same way. A ¾-inch skew was included for scale. (Photo courtesy of Woodcraft Supply)

Illus. 16-16. Finials are upright decorative elements, used on the top of clocks and case pieces, such as this secretary.

place on a piece of furniture by a screw, as is a drawer pull. Rather, they are held in place by gravity. Their tenons are fitted into a hole drilled into the top of the plinth. When turning the finial's tenon make sure that its diameter is great enough that the turning tool does not cut through to the screw.

Pendants can also be turned with a screw chuck. The word pendant is the present participle of the French verb *pendre*, which means "to hang." Thus, a pendant is something that is literally hanging. Pendants are less common than finials, but they can be found on Queen-Anne-period highboys and lowboys. (See Illus. 16-17.) They are made the same way as are

finials. The only difference in the way they are attached is that pendants have to be glued in place, and for that reason the stem should form a friction fit in its hole.

Corner blocks can be made with the screw chuck. In Greek Revival architecture, corner blocks were used at the upper corners of door and window casements. (See Illus. 16-18.) These blocks were sometimes decorated with turned rings. In this case, the rings are called *paterae*, after the Latin word for shield. Turned corner blocks remained popular throughout the Victorian period and well into the 20th century.

During those decades, turned discs called

Illus. 16-17. Pendants are hanging decorative elements, such as these elements on the skirt of a Queen Anne highboy.

Illus. 16-18. From the early 19th century well into the 20th, corner blocks were common architectural details on window and door casements.

rosettes were also commonly applied (glued or tacked to a flat surface) to such structures as stair newel posts and fireplace mantels. Beginning in the Federal period and throughout the rest of the 19th century, similar turned rosettes were also applied to furniture. When applied to furniture, these ornaments are also called *paterae* (singular, *patera*).

When making corner blocks, saw the block to either a square or rectangle, depending on the shape required. Locate the center on the rear surface by connecting the corners with an X. Drill a pilot hole as explained above, and screw the block to the chuck.

It may help to lay out the patera on the block's front surface while it is spinning. Use a #2 pencil. You can make up your own designs, copy an original, or use patterns found in catalogues of building materials printed during the Victorian period. Many of these have been reprinted, and I have included one in the bibliography. Illustrations of corner blocks are often accompanied by a cross section. If you are familiar with the architecture of that period, you will note that many of the paterae are turned with cross sections that are the same as those on Victorian moulding profiles.

Generally, a patera has a domed boss in the middle that is nearly the same thickness as the block. This prevents the turning tools from cut-

Illus. 16-19. Turn a corner block using a screw chuck.

Illus. 16-20. Rosettes are turned the same way, except that they are round rather than square.

ting through into the screw hole. Corner blocks are usually large enough so that the paterae can be turned with the turning tools that you use for general spindle work. (See Illus. 16-19.)

A rosette is turned the same way. Use the screw chuck to hold the blank. However, unlike a corner block, a rosette is round. Thus, cut the blank round on a band saw before mounting the chuck, or saw off the corners. This technique is explained in Chapter 15. Be sure to cut the blank so that it has a slightly larger diameter than the finished rosette, as you may lose some width bringing the outside edge into round. Once the rosette blank is round, turn the face as you would on a corner block. (See Illus. 16-20.)

BIBLIOGRAPHY

Benjamin, Asher. *American Builder's Companion.* New York: Dover Publishing Co., 1969.

Benjamin, Asher. *The Practical House Carpenter.* New York: Dover Publishing Co., 1969.

Dunbar, Michael. *Make a Windsor Chair With Michael Dunbar.* Newtown, CT: The Taunton Press Inc., 1984.

Holtzapffel, John Jacob. *Hand or Simple Turning: Principles & Practice.* New York: The Dover Publications, Inc., 1976.

Howells, John Mead. *The Architectural Heritage of the Piscataqua: Houses & Gardens of the Portsmouth District.* New York: Architectural Book Publishing Co., Inc., 1988.

Late Victorian Architectural Details. Watkins Glen, NY: American Life Foundation Study Institute, 1978.

Mayes, L. J. *The History of Chairmaking in High Wycombe.* London: Routledge & Kegan Paul Ltd., 1960.

Nutting, Wallace. *Furniture Treasury, Vol. III.* New York: The Macmillan Co., 1933.

Small, Tunstall and Woodbridge, Christopher. *Mouldings & Turned Woodwork of the 16th, 17th, and 18th Centuries.* Fresno, CA: Linden Publishing Co., 1977.

Woodbury, Robert S. *Studies in the History of Machine Tools.* Cambridge, MA and London, England: The M. I. T. Press, 1972.

Victorian Design Book. Ottawa, Ontario: Lee Valley Tools Ltd., 1984.

Metric Equivalents

INCHES TO MILLIMETRES AND CENTIMETRES

MM—millimetres   *CM—centimetres*

Inches	MM	CM	Inches	CM	Inches	CM
⅛	3	0.3	9	22.9	30	76.2
¼	6	0.6	10	25.4	31	78.7
⅜	10	1.0	11	27.9	32	81.3
½	13	1.3	12	30.5	33	83.8
⅝	16	1.6	13	33.0	34	86.4
¾	19	1.9	14	35.6	35	88.9
⅞	22	2.2	15	38.1	36	91.4
1	25	2.5	16	40.6	37	94.0
1¼	32	3.2	17	43.2	38	96.5
1½	38	3.8	18	45.7	39	99.1
1¾	44	4.4	19	48.3	40	101.6
2	51	5.1	20	50.8	41	104.1
2½	64	6.4	21	53.3	42	106.7
2	76	7.6	22	55.9	43	109.2
3½	89	8.9	23	58.4	44	111.8
4	102	10.2	24	61.0	45	114.3
4½	114	11.4	25	63.5	46	116.8
5	127	12.7	26	66.0	47	119.4
6	152	15.2	27	68.6	48	121.9
7	178	17.8	28	71.1	49	124.5
8	203	20.3	29	73.7	50	127.0

Index

for riving, 119–120
for turning, 20–26
Treadle lathe, 16–17
Treenware, 6
Turners, 6, 7
Turning
  definition of, 6
  green wood, 115–122
  history of, 6–7
  modern vs. old-time, 7–8
Turning squares
  center of, locating, 60–61
  method, 59
Turning tools, 20–26. *See also specific tools*

U
Urns, 73, 83–85

V
Vases, 73, 83
V grooves, 57
Vibration, 105–106

W
Waterstones, 34
Whetstones, 34
"Widow's walk," 110
Windsor chair leg
  examples of, 102, 104–105
  making, 105–108
Wood
  limitations of, 102–103
  species, determination of, 58–59